KERRY LORD

Alexandra's
GARDEN
FLOWERS

30 CROCHET FLOWER PATTERNS

#alexsgarden
@toft_uk

PAVILION

Contents

The Projects

Introduction

In stark contrast to my first book series, *Edward's Menagerie*, which was a frenzied rush of creativity from concept through to creation, *Alexandra's Garden Flowers* has been a very slow-growing and considered project, made over a couple of years. My crochet flower designs were entirely a product of the pandemic years, when we all had to turn to our own four walls and the spaces right outside our homes to find inspiration and entertainment. Like many, in 2020 I found a new love for soil and a suspicion of slugs that I never could have predicted. My two young children came on this journey with me, which started with one sunflower seed and has ended with a very large vegetable patch! Symbiotically my real garden and my crochet garden grew, inspiring each other every step of the way and with far more learning curves and experimentation than I had ever had in the creation of a book before.

The biggest challenge lay in the seasonality of the flowers and having to have them crocheted in the right colours at the right time to be able to capture the perfect pictures. With all my previous (and most) craft books, all the photography was done in one go, in a planned environment with controlled lighting. However, I was determined to make sure the pages of this book contained as many real flowers as crocheted ones, capturing exactly what inspired me and hoping to pass that on to readers. My 2020 involved lots of clearing of flowerbeds and planting of tubers and bulbs, before I crossed my fingers and hoped that real flowers matching the ones I had crocheted would pop up in 2021. In reality, my fingers took a while to turn green, and after lots of failed planting and learning more about composting and mulch than I care to mention, I stumbled across what would become my secret weapon – alpaca poo! The photography for the book was completed in 2022, and my garden is now bursting with colour, if planted up rather unusually to ensure that the photos could be taken easily with big clumps of a single bloom.

Early into the journey I realised that I needed a wider colour palette to work with, and that has produced a brand new range of TOFT pastel shades, named after the flowers that inspired them. TOFT is a company I started in 2006, with no idea of what it would grow to become. Our vision is to enrich the lives of as many people as possible with our shared love of craft, and our mission is to be as creative and original as possible, making products to inspire that in others. We specialise in luxury natural yarns and long-lasting, high-quality tools that come together in your hands to give you pleasure as you savour the feeling of making the stitches, and spread happiness with the results of your time. With this book, TOFT turns a new corner, with an entirely new range of designs and new colours to match. It combines two hobbies that give me a great deal of happiness.

I hope you enjoy cultivating these crochet patterns to create your own beautiful gardens from the comfort of your sofa as much as I did after those long days weeding!

How to use this book

The projects in this book are arranged in order of flowering throughout a year. Each project has a symbol (see below), showing you the skill level needed. Beginner projects will only require the basic stitches covered on pages 18–19, and easy and intermediate will require the advanced ones on pages 24–25. If you are a complete newcomer to crochet, then start with the Practice Bulb (page 26), and then I would recommend the Fuchsia or Poppy (pages 106 and 122) as great first flower projects. Once you've made one of these you will find it easy to progress onto whichever flower next takes your fancy.

If you are already a confident crocheter, dip in and out of the projects as you wish. Some designs use symbol charts for flat rather than 3D crochet pieces in addition to written instructions. If this is new to you, then refer to Reading a Chart on page 23.

All the standard stuffing and sewing up guidelines can be found on page 150. Unless otherwise stated in the pattern, once you have worked the last round of each pattern piece, gather the stitches to fasten off using the technique detailed on page 150. All pieces can be stuffed at the end, unless alternative instructions are provided in your pattern.

I have used British English crochet terms throughout. 'Double crochet' (dc) is the same as the American English 'single crochet' (sc). For clarification of all US terms and which stitches these refer to, see the table on page 24.

Skill level symbols

BEGINNER

EASY

INTERMEDIATE

Tools and materials

All of the flowers in this book were created using TOFT pure wool double knitting yarn on a 3mm aluminium hook, with a stuffing made from post-consumer recycled plastic bottles.

TOOLS

Hook
Choosing the right sized hook to match your yarn and create the correct tension is vital to guarantee the best results (see pages 16–17). If you are buying a hook for the first time, get a good-quality one with a comfortable handle as it also doubles as the perfect tool for pushing the toy stuffing inside arms and legs!

Stitch marker
Marking the start or end of your rounds when working this style of crochet is essential. I recommend using a piece of contrast yarn, approximately 15cm long, positioned in the last stitch of Round 2 in any piece. As you return around to your marker, pull it forwards or backwards through or between your stitches to mark the end of the round you have just finished, to help you keep track of where you are in the pattern. The marker will weave up the fabric with you, and you can pull it free at the end. Should you need to abandon your crochet halfway through a round, or if you lose your place, you will be able to return to your marker and avoid a total restart.

Centraliser
Use a lobster clip style stitch marker to mark the third increase in the body as you crochet. This will mark the centre of your body to help with sewing up and positioning your petals to the front.

Scissors
Sharp scissors or thread snips are ideal for snipping off ends at the surface of the fabric once secured.

Stuffing
Several types of stuffing are available, including natural pure wool and recycled synthetic options. Using a recycled polyester stuffing will make your flowers easier to wash by hand or in a cool cycle in the machine, and this tends to be a better option if they are being made as toys for children, but using all-natural materials guarantees they are one hundred percent compostable!

Sewing needle
Choose a sewing needle with a big enough eye so it is easy to thread with your yarn.

Contrast yarn or safety eyes
I used Cream and Black yarn to sew on all the flowers' eyes and the same technique can be used to add a smile. Safety eyes can be added before sewing up (however, they should not be used on a toy for a child under five).

Row counter
Use a row counter if following a pattern is a new discipline for you. It may make it easier to keep track of the pattern if you do not wish to mark your place in the book.

Project bag
Although not essential, a project bag can be very handy for keeping your latest make safe and in order.

Pins for sewing up
If you are new to 3D crochet, pins might help you position all the parts before sewing them together. While not essential, they can come in handy if you know that sewing legs in straight lines poses a challenge for your perfectionism.

YARN

I was inspired by TOFT yarn to learn to crochet and make these patterns, and they then inspired me to create six new pastel yarn colours to complete the collection. The yarns are named after the flowers that inspired them, so you'll come across Hyacinth, Primrose and Peony.

The quantity of yarn needed for the projects (based on TOFT pure wool double knit yarn) is stated in the table on the first page of each pattern. If using other brands of yarn, the quantities may vary significantly, depending on the fibre composition and spinning specifications of the yarn. For example, a cotton yarn will be heavier and you will require more of it, whereas an acrylic will be lighter and you will need less. When made in a TOFT double knitting yarn, the projects average 30cm from the bottom of their legs to the tip of the flower.

You can use these patterns with thinner or thicker yarns and thereby scale up or down to create bigger and smaller flowers, but be aware that you will require far more yarn for a bigger size, and some of the 'heads' of the flowers may end up very heavy as a result.

ABOUT TOFT

I have had the pleasure of selecting, designing and manufacturing luxury yarns for the past sixteen years as the founder of the TOFT brand. TOFT yarns are luxury, high-quality natural fibres manufactured to my distinctive specifications here in the UK. When crocheted in TOFT yarns, the projects in this book are supple and soft but with a closed fabric to hide the stuffing inside. Using natural fibres is not only better for the environment, but also ensures a beautiful finish, assures you that these flowers will only get better over time, whether made for display or to play with, and guarantees each stitch is a pleasure to make.

TOFT is based in a real place called Toft – in Warwickshire, England – and we are always here to help if you are new to crochet and not sure where to begin. In addition to our yarns, TOFT now designs and manufactures a whole range of tools and accessories to accompany the Alexandra's Garden crochet range. Video help is also on hand if you are struggling at any point with the techniques in this book. All materials, kits and videos for these projects are available at www.toftuk.com.

Colours

Alexandra's Garden has been created with a palette of three foliage colours, twelve flower colours, Cream and Black as base colours, and then a handful of natural browns for contrasts in seed heads. On the first page of every project I recommend alternative colours commonly seen in that type of flower. I very much look forward to these flowers being reimagined and crocheted into every colour combination imaginable to create specific species, and I will continue to experiment with new combinations myself. Remember that flowers take on symbolic meanings in specific colours, so choosing the right colour can make them even more perfect ways to send a message of love, friendship or solidarity. Read more about the colour symbolism of each flower in their introduction.

Flowers:
1. Peony
2. Pink
3. Magenta
4. Ruby
5. Violet
6. Amethyst
7. Hyacinth
8. Blue
9. Primrose
10. Yellow
11. Coral
12. Orange

Foliage:
13. Green
14. Lime
15. Sage

Base colours:
16. Cream
17. Black

Natural contrasts:
18. Mushroom
19. Chestnut
20. Fudge
21. Cocoa
22. Oatmeal

HAND-DYED YARN

Create the beauty of marbled colour variegation without the complexity of colour changing by using a hand-dyed yarn that combines several colours in one skein. This is particularly effective when used with the Peony, Tulip and Rose patterns and looks beautiful if used to create a bouquet of the same pattern.

Tension

The most important thing about making this style of stuffed crochet in double crochet stitch is to ensure that you are creating a closed fabric. If you are seeing holes in your fabric – and subsequently stuffing through your stitches – when working the patterns, swap your hook size down half a millimetre. Conversely, if your work is too solid and you are finding the stitches hard to work, then swap your hook size up half a millimetre. The arm shown opposite is at actual size, made using TOFT double knitting yarn and a 3mm hook. Use it to gauge your tension and adjust accordingly. If you find that this does not work, then take a look at the way you hold your hook and yarn and try to make a change to further impact your tension.

HOLDING YOUR HOOK

There are two principal ways of holding your crochet hook, one similar to holding a knife and the other to holding a pencil. If you are totally new to crochet, I would recommend the knife hold as it is easier to get comfortable with to maintain control and a good tension; if you already use the pencil hold successfully, then do not alter it, Even within these two holds there are lots of subtle variants, and there is no right or wrong way. Do what is most comfortable for you. If you are left-handed, there are no special changes you need to make as none of the patterns in this book refers to left and right. If it is necessary to clarify a direction of movement, I refer to your 'hook hand' or 'yarn hand'.

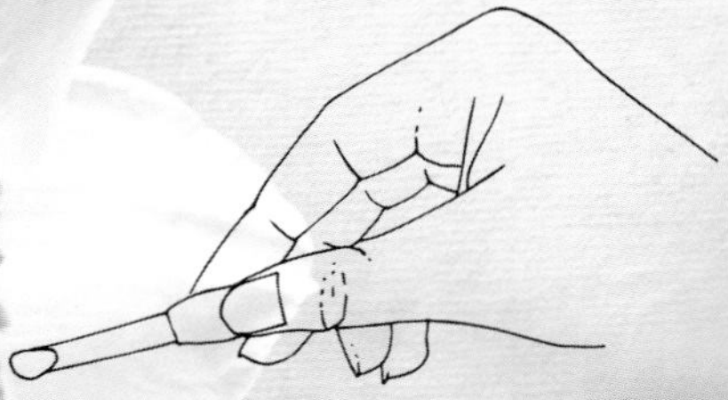

Knife hold

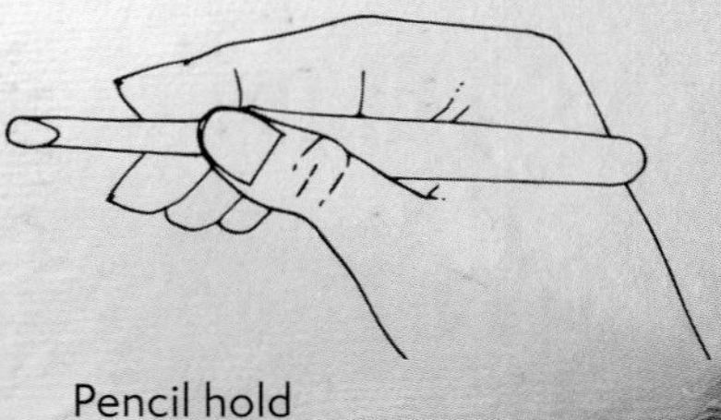

Pencil hold

HOLDING YOUR YARN

Every crocheter I meet holds their yarn in a
slightly different way, so use the illustrations
below as a rough guide and then
experiment with what is most comfortable
for you. Only adjust your hand position
if you think the way you hold the yarn is
causing a problem. Loose stitches can be
caused by not putting tension onto the yarn
coming off the ball by wrapping it around
your finger, but the opposite problem, of the
yarn not moving freely, can often be worse
and you will feel like you are fighting the
stitches and creating a very tight tension.

Right-handed hold

Left-handed hold

Learning to crochet (the basics)

Practise your hook and hand positions from the previous pages by working a long chain length. You will get used to coordinating both hands and find what works best for you. If you are managing to work the stitches and achieve the correct tension comfortably, then there is no right or wrong.

SLIP KNOT

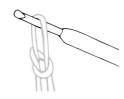

1 Wrap the yarn around your fingers.

2 Pull the tail end of the yarn through the wrap to make a loop.

3 Place your hook through the loop and tighten, ensuring that it is the tail end of the yarn (not the ball end) that controls the opening and closing of the knot.

CHAIN (CH)

1 Make a slipknot and place the loop on the hook.

2 Wrap the yarn over the hook (yarn over) and pull it through, keeping it close around the hook but not too tight.

3 Repeat until you reach the desired length (each repeat makes one chain).

DOUBLE CROCHET STITCH (DC)

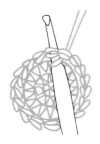

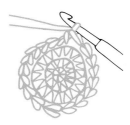

1 Insert the hook through the stitch under both loops of the 'V', unless otherwise stated.

2 Yarn over, the rotate hook head, and pull through the stitch (two loops on the hook).

3 Yarn over again and pull through both loops on the hook to end with one loop (one double crochet stitch made).

DC6 INTO RING (MAGIC CIRCLE)

1   Make a slipknot and chain two stitches.

2   Insert the hook into the first chain stitch made and work a double crochet six times into this same stitch.

3   Pull tightly on the tail of the yarn to close the centre of the ring and form a neat circle.

DECREASING (DC2TOG)

1   Insert the hook under the front loop only of the next stitch (two loops on the hook).

2   In the same motion, insert the hook through the front loop only of the following stitch (three loops on the hook).

3   Yarn over and pull through the first two loops on the hook, then yarn over again and pull through both remaining loops to complete the double crochet decrease.

CHANGING COLOUR

 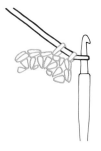 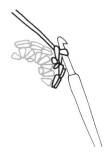

1   Insert the hook through the next stitch, yarn over and pull through the stitch (two loops on the hook).

2   Yarn over with the new colour and complete the double crochet stitch with this new yarn.

3   Continue with this new yarn, leaving the original yarn at the back of the work. Cut the original yarn if this is a one-off colour change, or run it along the back of the fabric if returning to it later.

19

Counting your stitches

An essential skill to keeping yourself on track and able to follow a pattern accurately is knowing how to count the number of stitches you have in a round. While learning, count your stitches in a round after each line of pattern that involves increasing or decreasing. The number in brackets at the end of a line of pattern indicates the number of stitches you should have once it is completed. If you complete a round and this number is wrong, then pull back your work to the beginning of the round and redo it until you have the correct number of stitches before you progress – this is much easier with a stitch marker (see page 10).

COUNTING THE STITCHES IN A ROUND

Your crochet piece will grow from a set number of stitches in a closed ring (usually six). The piece you are making grows because you are increasing the number of stitches by sometimes working two double crochet stitches into the same stitch, as instructed.

When working the style of crochet used in this book to create a solid fabric and 3D shapes, you generally start from a closed ring and work the double crochet stitch in one direction in a non-stop spiral. The pattern for the start of the head of most flowers forms a pretty standard increase for this style of crochet by adding six stitches evenly into every round. The piece becomes 3D once you stop adding six stitches into a round.

RIGHT SIDE (RS) AND WRONG SIDE (WS)

If you are new to this style of crochet, you do need to be aware that there is a right side (RS) and wrong side (WS) to the fabric; the wrong side forms the inside of the shape. If you are right-handed and crocheting with the RS facing outwards, you will be moving in an anti-clockwise direction around the edge of the circle of fabric (left-handed people will be moving clockwise). It is very easy to have learned to crochet holding the WS facing outwards (I did so myself); this will mean that your resulting piece is inside out when you come to stuff and finish it. With some parts this will not be a problem, as you can simply flip them before stuffing and sewing up. However, with the parts containing smaller rounds, such as Sunflower petals, this will be impossible, so it is best to adjust your hold to ensure you are crocheting into the RS of the fabric, with the RS on the outside of the 3D shape. On the RS of the fabric you will see the rounds horizontally on the piece. On the WS you can see vertical furrows spiralling up the piece (see photos, right).

COUNTING A CHAIN

When you crochet a chain and then work back down it, you will often miss the stitch closest to the hook in order to turn. For example, you might chain ten stitches in order to double crochet nine stitches back down the chain.

Reading a pattern

RND: ROUND
A round is a complete rotation in a spiral back to where you started. In this style of crochet you DO NOT slip stitch at the end of a round to make a circle, but instead continue directly on to the next round in a spiral.

ARMS (make two)
Ch12 and sl st to join into a circle

Rnds 1–20 dc (20 rnds)

Rnd 21 (dc5, dc2 into next st) twice (14)

Rnd 22 (dc6, dc2 into next st) twice (16)

Rnd 23 (dc7, dc2 into next st) twice (18)

Rnds 24–29 dc (6 rnds)

Rnd 30 (dc7, dc2tog) twice (16)

Rnd 31 (dc6, dc2tog) twice (14)

Rnd 32 (dc5, dc2tog) twice (12)

Rnd 33 (dc4, dc2tog) twice (10)

Rnd 34 (dc3, dc2tog) twice (8)

Rnd 35 (dc2, dc2tog) twice (6)

Rnd 36 (dc1, dc2tog) twice (4)

Stuff end lightly and sew flat across top to close.

20 RNDS
Work one double crochet stitch into every stitch in the round for twenty full rounds.

2 TIMES
Repeat what comes directly before this instruction within the brackets the number of times stated.

STITCH COUNT
The number in brackets at the end of a line indicates the number of stitches in that round once it has been completed.

DC: DOUBLE CROCHET
Dc5 means to double crochet one stitch into each of the next five stitches.

CHAIN AND THEN SL ST TO JOIN INTO A CIRCLE

1 Chain the stated number of stitches, then insert the hook into the stitch closest to the slipknot, taking care not to twist the stitches.

2 Yarn over the hook.

3 Pull the yarn through the stitch and the loop on the hook in one motion.

Reading a chart

Sometimes you will find that a pattern includes a chart, which you can use to help you visualise what you are making. Using the key below, follow the graphic from either the starting chain or foundation ring. If crocheting left handed, the chart would be worked in mirror image. A new row or round will be indicated by a change of colour in the chart.

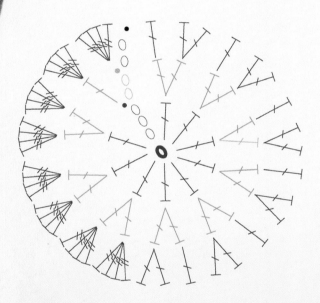

⟲	FOUNDATION RING (X STS INTO RING)	+	DOUBLE CROCHET (DC)
⬭	STARTING CHAIN	T	HALF TREBLE CROCHET (HTR)
⬭	CHAIN (CH)	Ŧ	TREBLE CROCHET (TR)
●	SLIP STITCH (SL ST)	ǂ	DOUBLE TREBLE CROCHET (DTR)

Learning to crochet (advanced stitches)

A reminder that this book uses British English crochet terms. See the key below for US terms.

UK		US	
ch	chain	ch	chain
sl st	slip stitch	sl st	slip stitch
dc	double crochet	sc	single crochet
dc2tog	dc 2 together	sc2tog	sc 2 together
htr	half treble crochet	hdc	half double crochet
tr	treble crochet	dc	double crochet
dtr (also ttr, qtr)	double treble crochet	tr	treble crochet
ttr	triple treble crochet	dtr	double treble crochet
qtr	quadruple treble crochet	ttr	triple treble crochet

HALF TREBLE CROCHET STITCH (HTR)

1 Yarn over and insert the hook into the next stitch.

2 Yarn over and pull through the stitch (three loops on the hook).

3 Yarn over and pull through all three loops on the hook (one half treble crochet stitch made).

TREBLE CROCHET STITCH (TR)

1 Yarn over and insert the hook into the next stitch.

2 Yarn over and pull through the stitch (three loops on hook), then yarn over again and pull through the first two loops on the hook (two loops on the hook).

3 Yarn over again and pull through the remaining two loops on the hook (one treble crochet stitch made).

DOUBLE TREBLE CROCHET STITCH (DTR, TTR, QTR)

1 Yarn over twice and insert the hook into the next stitch.

2 Yarn over and pull through the stitch (four loops on the hook), then yarn over again and pull through the two loops on the hook (three loops on the hook); repeat again until there are two loops on the hook.

3 Yarn over again and pull through the remaining two loops on the hook (one double treble crochet stitch made). NB: for the triple treble (ttr) wrap one extra time in step one. Similarly, for the qtr wrap twice more.

Practice bulb

If you are new to crochet, or if you'd simply like a warm-up, try this little bulb to master all the basic techniques as well as a couple of others – plus your first set of embroidered eyes. The arms will be the most challenging if you are new to crochet, as they are more fiddly, but if you can master these then you will be ready to make any of the 'EASY' flowers in this book.

YOU WILL NEED
3mm crochet hook and 25g of two colours of double knitting wool (shown here in Cream and Fudge)

BULB/BODY
Working in Fudge
Begin by dc3 into ring
Rnd 1 dc (3 sts)
Rnd 2 (dc2 into next st) 3 times (6)
Rnd 3 (dc2, dc2 into next st) twice (8)
Rnd 4 (dc3, dc2 into next st) twice (10)
Rnd 5 (dc4, dc2 into next st) twice (12)
Rnd 6 (dc1, dc2 into next st) 6 times (18)
Rnd 7 (dc2, dc2 into next st) 6 times (24)
Rnd 8 (dc3, dc2 into next st) 6 times (30)
Rnd 9 dc
Rnd 10 (dc4, dc2 into next st) 6 times (36)
Rnds 11–13 dc (3 rnds)
Rnd 14 (dc4, dc2tog) 6 times (30)
Rnd 15 dc
Rnd 16 (dc3, dc2tog) 6 times (24)
Rnd 17 (dc2, dc2tog) 6 times (18)
Rnd 18 (dc2tog) 9 times (9)
Stuff and change to Cream
Rnd 19 dc
Rnd 20 (dc2, dc2 into next st) 3 times (12)
Rnd 21 (dc3, dc2 into next st) 3 times (15)
Rnds 22–24 dc (3 rnds)
Rnd 25 (dc4, dc2 into next st) 3 times (18)
Rnd 26 (dc2 into next st) 6 times, dc12 (24)
Rnd 27 (dc3, dc2 into next st) 6 times (30)
Rnds 28–30 dc (3 rnds)
Rnd 31 (dc1, dc2tog) 10 times (20)
Rnd 32 (dc3, dc2tog) 4 times (16)
Rnd 33 (dc2tog) 8 times (8)

When you have finished the end of every piece, simply cut the yarn, leaving 8–10cm for sewing up. Pull the end through the loop on your hook. Remove the hook and pull on the end to tighten.

Stuff the bottom of the bulb and gather the sts (see page 150), then work the stem roots directly onto the bottom.

STEM ROOTS
Working in Cream
Sl st into fabric on base of Cream piece
*Ch18, turn and work back down chain as follows:
sl st5, dc3 into next st, htr5, dc2tog, tr4, sl st into body
Repeat from * to make seven roots around the bottom of the body.

ARMS (make two)
Working in Cream
Ch8 and sl st to join into a circle
Rnds 1–5 dc (5 rnds)
Rnd 6 dc2tog, dc6 (7)
Rnds 7–9 dc (3 rnds)
Rnd 10 dc2tog, dc5 (6)
Rnds 11–13 dc (3 rnds)
Rnd 14 dc2tog, dc4 (5)
Rnd 15 dc2tog, dc3 (4)
Gather sts to close.
Do not stuff.
Sew into position on either side of the 'neck'.
Finish by sewing the eyes and mouth into place with Black and Cream yarn.

The
PROJECTS

Winter Aconite

Through the heavy frosts and shallow drifts of snow in January you'll find the very first green shoots of the year. The early flowering yellow heads of the 'winter buttercup', with its unusual green ruff, peep up to give hope of the change of seasons. Growing in a wild clump at the bottom of the bare cherry tree, Winter Aconite is the only flower adding colour to my Winter garden as I patiently wait for the rest of the green shoots of Spring.

HEAD/BODY

Working in Yellow
Begin by dc6 into ring
Rnd 1 (dc2 into next st) 6 times (12 sts)
Rnd 2 dc
Rnd 3 (dc1, dc2 into next st) 6 times (18)
Rnd 4 dc
Rnd 5 (dc2, dc2 into next st) 6 times (24)
Rnd 6 dc
Rnd 7 (dc3, dc2 into next st) 6 times (30)
Rnd 8 dc
Rnd 9 (dc4, dc2 into next st) 6 times (36)
Rnd 10 (dc5, dc2 into next st) 6 times (42)
Rnd 11 (dc6, dc2 into next st) 6 times (48)
Rnd 12 (dc7, dc2 into next st) 6 times (54)
Rnds 13–17 dc (5 rnds)
Rnd 18 (dc7, dc2tog) 6 times (48)
Rnd 19 (dc6, dc2tog) 6 times (42)
Rnd 20 (dc5, dc2tog) 6 times (36)
Rnd 21 (dc4, dc2tog) 6 times (30)
Rnd 22 (dc3, dc2tog) 6 times (24)
Rnd 23 (dc2, dc2tog) 6 times (18)
Rnd 24 (dc2tog) 9 times (9)
Change to Green
Rnds 25–26 dc (2 rnds)

Rnd 27 (dc2 into next st) 9 times (18)
Rnd 28 (dc2, dc2 into next st) 6 times (24)
Rnds 29–34 dc (6 rnds)
Rnd 35 (dc3, dc2 into next st) 6 times (30)
Rnds 36–38 dc (3 rnds)
Rnd 39 (dc4, dc2 into next st) 6 times (36)
Rnd 40 dc12, (dc1, dc2 into next st) 6 times, dc12 (42)
Rnd 41 (dc6, dc2 into next st) 6 times (48)
Rnds 42–46 dc (5 rnds)
Rnd 47 (dc6, dc2tog) 6 times (42)
Rnd 48 (dc5, dc2tog) 6 times (36)
Rnd 49 dc
Rnd 50 (dc4, dc2tog) 6 times (30)
Rnd 51 (dc3, dc2tog) 6 times (24)
Rnd 52 (dc2, dc2tog) 6 times (18)
Rnd 53 (dc2tog) 9 times (9)

ARMS/LEGS (make four)

Working in Green
Ch12 and sl st to join into a circle
Rnds 1–35 dc (35 rnds)
Rnd 36 (dc2tog) 6 times (6)
Stuff end and sew flat across top to close.
Continues overleaf

MADE IN Green and Yellow
YARN QUANTITIES 100g foliage, 25g flower
TIME TO GROW Moderate
COLOUR VARIANTS None
REQUIRES Splitting the round

COLLAR
Working in Green

CENTRE (make two)
Ch12 and sl st to join into a circle
Rnd 1 (dc1, dc2 into next st) 6 times (18)
Rnd 2 (dc2, dc2 into next st) 6 times (24)
Rnd 3 (dc3, dc2 into next st) 6 times (30)
Rnd 4 (dc4, dc2 into next st) 6 times (36)

Place both pieces together with RS facing
    outwards.
Continue to work a total of six 12-st rnds
    around edge of CENTRE by working 6 sts
    from each piece to create the rnd.

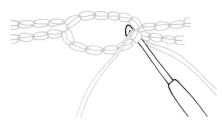

Work each 12-st rnd as follows:
Rnds 1–3 dc (3 rnds)
Split into two rnds of 6 sts and rejoin and work
    each as follows:

Rnds 1–4 dc (4 rnds)
Rnd 5 (dc1, dc2 into next st) 3 times (9)
Rnd 6 dc
Rnd 7 (dc1, dc2tog) 3 times (6)

Break yarn and rejoin to work second set of
    6 sts as first.

Repeat step 2 five more times.

Insert head into collar before stuffing (see page
    155).

Finish by sewing eyes into place with Black and
    Cream yarn.

Snowdrop

Fans of a cold Winter, snowdrops lie asleep in the soil all Summer waiting to brighten the first months of the year with bright lime shoots. Beloved for their delicate beauty, they have taken on rich cultural symbolism over time. Associated with purity, hope and sympathy, snowdrops are written into myth and stories as far back as Homer's *Odyssey*, where these pure white flowers are used to clear Odysseus's mind of witchcraft. A brilliant metaphor for new life and regeneration, and a flower that can express hope and dreams.

HEAD/BODY

Working in Cream

Begin by dc6 into ring

Rnd 1 (dc2 into next st) 6 times (12 sts)
Rnd 2 (dc1, dc2 into next st) 6 times (18)
Rnd 3 (dc2, dc2 into next st) 6 times (24)
Rnd 4 (dc3, dc2 into next st) 6 times (30)
Rnd 5 (dc4, dc2 into next st) 6 times (36)
Rnd 6 (dc5, dc2 into next st) 6 times (42)
Rnd 7 (dc6, dc2 into next st) 6 times (48)
Rnd 8 (dc7, dc2 into next st) 6 times (54)
Rnds 9–13 dc (5 rnds)
Rnd 14 (dc7, dc2tog) 6 times (48)
Rnd 15 (dc6, dc2tog) 6 times (42)
Rnd 16 (dc5, dc2tog) 6 times (36)
Rnd 17 (dc4, dc2tog) 6 times (30)
Rnd 18 (dc3, dc2tog) 6 times (24)
Rnd 19 (dc2, dc2tog) 6 times (18)
Rnd 20 (dc2tog) 9 times (9)
Change to Lime
Rnds 21–22 dc (2 rnds)
Rnd 23 (dc2 into next st) 9 times (18)
Rnd 24 (dc2, dc2 into next st) 6 times (24)
Rnds 25–30 dc (6 rnds)

Rnd 31 (dc3, dc2 into next st) 6 times (30)
Rnds 32–34 dc (3 rnds)
Rnd 35 (dc4, dc2 into next st) 6 times (36)
Rnd 36 dc12, (dc1, dc2 into next st) 6 times, dc12 (42)
Rnd 37 (dc6, dc2 into next st) 6 times (48)
Rnds 38–42 dc (5 rnds)
Rnd 43 (dc6, dc2tog) 6 times (42)
Rnd 44 (dc5, dc2tog) 6 times (36)
Rnd 45 dc
Rnd 46 (dc4, dc2tog) 6 times (30)
Rnd 47 (dc3, dc2tog) 6 times (24)
Rnd 48 (dc2, dc2tog) 6 times (18)
Rnd 49 (dc2tog) 9 times (9)

ARMS (make two)

Working in Lime

Ch12 and sl st to join into a circle

Rnds 1–20 dc (20 rnds)
Rnd 21 (dc5, dc2 into next st) twice (14)
Rnd 22 (dc6, dc2 into next st) twice (16)
Rnd 23 (dc7, dc2 into next st) twice (18)
Rnds 24–29 dc (6 rnds)
Continues overleaf

MADE IN Lime and Cream
YARN QUANTITIES 75g foliage, 75g flower
TIME TO GROW Slow grower
COLOUR VARIANTS None
REQUIRES Just the basics!

Rnd 30 (dc7, dc2tog) twice (16)
Rnd 31 (dc6, dc2tog) twice (14)
Rnd 32 (dc5, dc2tog) twice (12)
Rnd 33 (dc4, dc2tog) twice (10)
Rnd 34 (dc3, dc2tog) twice (8)
Rnd 35 (dc2, dc2tog) twice (6)
Rnd 36 (dc1, dc2tog) twice (4)
Stuff end lightly and sew flat across top
    to close.

LEGS (make two)

Working in Lime
Ch12 and sl st to join into a circle
Rnds 1–35 dc (35 rnds)
Rnd 36 (dc2tog) 6 times (6)
Stuff foot and sew flat across top to close.

BOTTOM PETAL

Working in Cream
Begin by dc6 into ring
Rnd 1 (dc2 into next st) 6 times (12)
Rnd 2 (dc3, dc2 into next st) 3 times (15)
Rnd 3 (dc4, dc2 into next st) 3 times (18)
Rnd 4 (dc5, dc2 into next st) 3 times (21)
Rnd 5 (dc6, dc2 into next st) 3 times (24)
Rnd 6 (dc7, dc2 into next st) 3 times (27)
Rnd 7 (dc8, dc2 into next st) 3 times (30)
Rnd 8 dc
Rnd 9 (dc4, dc2 into next st) 6 times (36)
Rnds 10–17 dc (8 rnds)
Rnd 18 (dc2tog, dc4) 6 times (30)
Rnd 19 dc
Rnd 20 (dc2tog, dc3) 6 times (24)
Rnds 21–25 dc (5 rnds)
Rnd 26 (dc6, dc2tog) 3 times (21)
Rnds 27–29 dc (3 rnds)
Rnd 30 (dc2 into next st, dc2) 7 times (28)
Do not stuff.

TOP PETALS (make two)

Working in Cream
Begin by dc6 into ring

Rnd 1 (dc2 into next st) 6 times (12)
Rnd 2 (dc3, dc2 into next st) 3 times (15)
Rnd 3 (dc4, dc2 into next st) 3 times (18)
Rnd 4 (dc5, dc2 into next st) 3 times (21)
Rnd 5 (dc6, dc2 into next st) 3 times (24)
Rnd 6 (dc7, dc2 into next st) 3 times (27)
Rnd 7 (dc8, dc2 into next st) 3 times (30)
Rnd 8 dc
Rnd 9 (dc4, dc2 into next st) 6 times (36)
Rnds 10–17 dc (8 rnds)
Rnd 18 (dc2tog, dc4) 6 times (30)
Rnd 19 dc
Rnd 20 (dc2tog, dc3) 6 times (24)
Rnds 21–25 dc (5 rnds)
Rnd 26 (dc6, dc2tog) 3 times (21)
Rnds 27–32 dc (6 rnds)
Rnd 33 (dc2 into next st, dc2) 7 times (28)
Do not stuff.

Make a ring of petals by dc along bottom of
    each petal.
Sew into position on head (see pages 152–153).

HOOD

Working in Lime
Begin by dc6 into ring
Rnd 1 (dc2 into next st) 6 times (12)
Rnd 2 (dc1, dc2 into next st) 6 times (18)
Rnd 3 dc
Rnd 4 (dc2, dc2 into next st) 6 times (24)
Rnd 5 dc
Rnd 6 (dc3, dc2 into next st) 6 times (30)
Rnd 7 (dc4, dc2 into next st) 6 times (36)
Rnd 8 (dc5, dc2 into next st) 6 times (42)
Rnd 9 (dc6, dc2 into next st) 6 times (48)
Rnds 10–12 dc (3 rnds)
Rnd 13 dc42, ch6, miss 6 sts and put hood
    onto back of head with ch6 going across
    front of neck and sl st to secure.

Finish by sewing eyes into place with Black and
    Cream yarn.

Crocus

Humans have been cultivating crocuses for 3000 years, gathering the stigmas to produce saffron for spice and dye. As an early Spring flower it has lots of associations with regeneration and rebirth, but other symbolism goes back to Ancient Greece. Due to its bold flowers heralding the end of Winter, the crocus has also more generally become a symbol of an end to hardship and a promise of hope. Additionally, white crocuses embody truth, grace and spirituality, while purple crocuses are symbols of success and power. The gift of a classic yellow crocus, like many other yellow flowers, is guaranteed to give the recipient a sense of joy and optimism.

HEAD/BODY
Working in Yellow
Begin by dc6 into ring
Rnd 1 (dc2 into next st) 6 times (12 sts)
Rnd 2 (dc1, dc2 into next st) 6 times (18)
Rnd 3 (dc2, dc2 into next st) 6 times (24)
Rnd 4 (dc3, dc2 into next st) 6 times (30)
Rnd 5 (dc4, dc2 into next st) 6 times (36)
Rnd 6 (dc5, dc2 into next st) 6 times (42)
Rnd 7 (dc6, dc2 into next st) 6 times (48)
Rnd 8 (dc7, dc2 into next st) 6 times (54)
Rnds 9–13 dc (5 rnds)
Rnd 14 (dc7, dc2tog) 6 times (48)
Rnd 15 (dc6, dc2tog) 6 times (42)
Rnd 16 (dc5, dc2tog) 6 times (36)
Rnd 17 (dc4, dc2tog) 6 times (30)
Rnd 18 (dc3, dc2tog) 6 times (24)
Rnd 19 (dc2, dc2tog) 6 times (18)
Rnd 20 (dc2tog) 9 times (9)
Change to Lime
Rnds 21–22 dc (2 rnds)
Rnd 23 (dc2 into next st) 9 times (18)

Rnd 24 (dc2, dc2 into next st) 6 times (24)
Rnds 25–30 dc (6 rnds)
Rnd 31 (dc3, dc2 into next st) 6 times (30)
Rnds 32–34 dc (3 rnds)
Rnd 35 (dc4, dc2 into next st) 6 times (36)
Rnd 36 dc12, (dc1, dc2 into next st) 6 times, dc12 (42)
Rnd 37 (dc6, dc2 into next st) 6 times (48)
Rnds 38–42 dc (5 rnds)
Rnd 43 (dc6, dc2tog) 6 times (42)
Rnd 44 (dc5, dc2tog) 6 times (36)
Rnd 45 dc
Rnd 46 (dc4, dc2tog) 6 times (30)
Rnd 47 (dc3, dc2tog) 6 times (24)
Rnd 48 (dc2, dc2tog) 6 times (18)
Rnd 49 (dc2tog) 9 times (9)

ARMS (make two)
Working in Lime
Ch12 and sl st to join into a circle
Rnds 1–20 dc (20 rnds)
Continues overleaf

MADE IN Lime, Violet and Yellow (overleaf with Amethyst flowers)
YARN QUANTITIES 50g foliage, 25g flower, 25g flower contrast and 25g stigma
TIME TO GROW Speedy grower
COLOUR VARIANTS Violet, Cream, Yellow, Ruby, Pink
REQUIRES Just the basics!

Rnd 21 (dc5, dc2 into next st) twice (14)
Rnd 22 (dc6, dc2 into next st) twice (16)
Rnd 23 (dc7, dc2 into next st) twice (18)
Rnds 24–29 dc (6 rnds)
Rnd 30 (dc7, dc2tog) twice (16)
Rnd 31 (dc6, dc2tog) twice (14)
Rnd 32 (dc5, dc2tog) twice (12)
Rnd 33 (dc4, dc2tog) twice (10)
Rnd 34 (dc3, dc2tog) twice (8)
Rnd 35 (dc2, dc2tog) twice (6)
Rnd 36 (dc1, dc2tog) twice (4)
Stuff end lightly and sew flat across top
   to close.

LEGS (make two)
Working in Lime
Ch12 and sl st to join into a circle
Rnds 1–35 dc (35 rnds)
Rnd 36 (dc2tog) 6 times (6)
Stuff foot and sew flat across top to close.

FLOWER HOOD
Working in Violet
Ch15 and sl st to join into a circle
Rnd 1 (dc4, dc2 into next st) 3 times (18)
Rnd 2 (dc2, dc2 into next st) 6 times (24)
Rnd 3 (dc3, dc2 into next st) 6 times (30)
Rnd 4 (dc4, dc2 into next st) 6 times (36)

Rnd 5 dc
Rnd 6 (dc5, dc2 into next st) 6 times (42)
Rnd 7 dc
Rnd 8 (dc6, dc2 into next st) 6 times (48)
Rnds 9–16 dc (8 rnds)
*dc16, ch14, count back 16 sts and sl st to
   create a 30-st round. Work as follows:
Rnds 1–4 dc (4 rnds)
Rnd 5 (dc3, dc2tog) 6 times (24)
Rnd 6 (dc2, dc2tog) 6 times (18)
Rnd 7 (dc1, dc2tog) 6 times (12)
Rnd 8 (dc2tog) 6 times (6)
Break yarn.
Rejoin and repeat from * twice more to create
   three petals in total.

Add flower hood before stuffing (see page 155).

STIGMA
Working in Yellow
Work three chains around centre top of head
   as follows:
*sl st into position on top of head, ch9, turn
   and dc8 back down ch
Repeat from * twice more

Finish by sewing eyes into place with Black and
   Cream yarn.

Primrose

Another early sign that Winter is over, these originally wild delicate flowers can be found in shady, damp areas of the Spring garden. Featuring heavily across the myths and folklore of different cultures, the primrose signifies protection, safety and new or young love. The flowers figure in Norse mythology as a symbol of Freya, the goddess of love, their pale yellow colour representing her fairness. The ancient Celts believed that large patches of flowering primroses were gateways into the realm of the fairies and that placing primroses on a doorstep would encourage magic folk to bless a house and its inhabitants.

HEAD/BODY
Working in Yellow
Begin by dc6 into ring
Rnd 1 (dc2 into next st) 6 times (12 sts)
Rnd 2 (dc1, dc2 into next st) 6 times (18)
Rnd 3 (dc2, dc2 into next st) 6 times (24)
Rnd 4 (dc3, dc2 into next st) 6 times (30)
Rnd 5 (dc4, dc2 into next st) 6 times (36)
Rnd 6 (dc5, dc2 into next st) 6 times (42)
Rnd 7 (dc6, dc2 into next st) 6 times (48)
Rnd 8 (dc7, dc2 into next st) 6 times (54)
Rnds 9–13 dc (5 rnds)
Rnd 14 (dc7, dc2tog) 6 times (48)
Rnd 15 (dc6, dc2tog) 6 times (42)
Rnd 16 (dc5, dc2tog) 6 times (36)
Rnd 17 (dc4, dc2tog) 6 times (30)
Rnd 18 (dc3, dc2tog) 6 times (24)
Rnd 19 (dc2, dc2tog) 6 times (18)
Rnd 20 (dc2tog) 9 times (9)
Change to Green
Rnds 21–22 dc (2 rnds)
Rnd 23 (dc2 into next st) 9 times (18)
Rnd 24 (dc2, dc2 into next st) 6 times (24)

Rnds 25–30 dc (6 rnds)
Rnd 31 (dc3, dc2 into next st) 6 times (30)
Rnds 32–34 dc (3 rnds)
Rnd 35 (dc4, dc2 into next st) 6 times (36)
Rnd 36 dc12, (dc1, dc2 into next st) 6 times, dc12 (42)
Rnd 37 (dc6, dc2 into next st) 6 times (48)
Rnds 38–42 dc (5 rnds)
Rnd 43 (dc6, dc2tog) 6 times (42)
Rnd 44 (dc5, dc2tog) 6 times (36)
Rnd 45 dc
Rnd 46 (dc4, dc2tog) 6 times (30)
Rnd 47 (dc3, dc2tog) 6 times (24)
Rnd 48 (dc2, dc2tog) 6 times (18)
Rnd 49 (dc2tog) 9 times (9)

ARMS (make two)
Working in Green
Ch12 and sl st to join into a circle
Rnds 1–20 dc (20 rnds)
Rnd 21 (dc5, dc2 into next st) twice (14)
Rnd 22 (dc6, dc2 into next st) twice (16)
Continues overleaf

MADE IN Green, Primrose and Yellow
YARN QUANTITIES 50g foliage, 75g flower, 25g flower contrast
TIME TO GROW Moderate
COLOUR VARIANTS Cream, Peony, Magenta, Blue, Amethyst
REQUIRES htr, tr, dtr, ttr, splitting the round (see illustration 2, page 33), slip stitch traverse

Rnd 23 (dc7, dc2 into next st) twice (18)
Rnds 24–29 dc (6 rnds)
Rnd 30 (dc7, dc2tog) twice (16)
Rnd 31 (dc6, dc2tog) twice (14)
Rnd 32 (dc5, dc2tog) twice (12)
Rnd 33 (dc4, dc2tog) twice (10)
Rnd 34 (dc3, dc2tog) twice (8)
Rnd 35 (dc2, dc2tog) twice (6)
Rnd 36 (dc1, dc2tog) twice (4)
Stuff end lightly and sew flat across top
   to close.

LEGS (make two)
Working in Green
Ch12 and sl st to join into a circle
Rnds 1–35 dc (35 rnds)
Rnd 36 (dc2tog) 6 times (6)
Stuff foot and sew flat across top to close.

PETALS (make five)
Working in Primrose
Begin by dc6 into ring
Rnd 1 (dc2 into next st) 6 times (12)
Rnd 2 (dc1, dc2 into next st) 6 times (18)
Rnd 3 dc
Rnd 4 (dc5, dc2 into next st) 3 times (21)
Rnd 5 (dc6, dc2 into next st) 3 times (24)
Rnds 6–7 dc (2 rnds)

Rnd 8 (dc3, dc2 into next st) 6 times (30)
Rnds 9–11 dc (3 rnds)
Split into two rnds of 15 sts and work each
   as follows:
Rnd 1 dc
Rnd 2 (dc3, dc2tog) 3 times (12)
Rnd 3 (dc2tog) 6 times (6)

Rejoin and work 2 rnds dc around edge of
   each petal with a sl st at nape of heart.

Make a ring of petals by dc5 along bottom of
   each petal with a ch3 in between each petal.
Sew into position on head (see pages 152–153).

Sl st onto bottom corner of one petal, ch8 and
   sl st to centre of petal 8 rnds up.
Work back down chain as follows:
Sl st 1, dc1, htr1, tr1, dtr1, trtr2, sl st into other
   side of petal. SLIP STITCH TRAVERSE (see
   page 154) 2 sts along head and then sl st into
   bottom of next petal.
Repeat for all petals.

Finish by sewing eyes into place with Black and
   Cream yarn.

Daffodil

Daffodils represent truth and honesty, kind regard and chivalry, and are an excellent flower to give when apologising to someone. Daffodils are thought to have been the favourite flower of Queen Anne, which inspired her to build the first botanical garden in England, commonly known today as Kensington Palace Gardens. Although now the national symbol of Wales, daffodils are not native to the UK. Another early Spring flower, in their many forms they are indicative of rebirth, new beginnings and eternal life. Some say a single daffodil foretells a misfortune, whereas a bunch of daffodils signifies joy and happiness, so get ready to crochet a whole vase full!

HEAD/BODY
Working in Yellow
Begin by dc6 into ring
Rnd 1 (dc2 into next st) 6 times (12 sts)
Rnd 2 (dc1, dc2 into next st) 6 times (18)
Rnd 3 (dc2, dc2 into next st) 6 times (24)
Rnd 4 (dc3, dc2 into next st) 6 times (30)
Rnd 5 (dc4, dc2 into next st) 6 times (36)
Rnd 6 (dc5, dc2 into next st) 6 times (42)
Rnd 7 (dc6, dc2 into next st) 6 times (48)
Rnd 8 (dc7, dc2 into next st) 6 times (54)
Rnds 9–13 dc (5 rnds)
Rnd 14 (dc7, dc2tog) 6 times (48)
Rnd 15 (dc6, dc2tog) 6 times (42)
Rnd 16 (dc5, dc2tog) 6 times (36)
Rnd 17 (dc4, dc2tog) 6 times (30)
Rnd 18 (dc3, dc2tog) 6 times (24)
Rnd 19 (dc2, dc2tog) 6 times (18)
Rnd 20 (dc2tog) 9 times (9)
Change to Lime
Rnds 21–22 dc (2 rnds)
Rnd 23 (dc2 into next st) 9 times (18)

Rnd 24 (dc2, dc2 into next st) 6 times (24)
Rnds 25–30 dc (6 rnds)
Rnd 31 (dc3, dc2 into next st) 6 times (30)
Rnds 32–34 dc (3 rnds)
Rnd 35 (dc4, dc2 into next st) 6 times (36)
Rnd 36 dc12, (dc1, dc2 into next st) 6 times, dc12 (42)
Rnd 37 (dc6, dc2 into next st) 6 times (48)
Rnds 38–42 dc (5 rnds)
Rnd 43 (dc6, dc2tog) 6 times (42)
Rnd 44 (dc5, dc2tog) 6 times (36)
Rnd 45 dc
Rnd 46 (dc4, dc2tog) 6 times (30)
Rnd 47 (dc3, dc2tog) 6 times (24)
Rnd 48 (dc2, dc2tog) 6 times (18)
Rnd 49 (dc2tog) 9 times (9)

ARMS (make two)
Working in Lime
Ch12 and sl st to join into a circle
Rnds 1–20 dc (20 rnds)
Continues overleaf

MADE IN Lime, Primrose and Yellow
YARN QUANTITIES 50g foliage, 50g flower, 25g flower contrast
TIME TO GROW Moderate
COLOUR VARIANTS Primrose, Orange
REQUIRES Just the basics!

Rnd 21 (dc5, dc2 into next st) twice (14)
Rnd 22 (dc6, dc2 into next st) twice (16)
Rnd 23 (dc7, dc2 into next st) twice (18)
Rnds 24–29 dc (6 rnds)
Rnd 30 (dc7, dc2tog) twice (16)
Rnd 31 (dc6, dc2tog) twice (14)
Rnd 32 (dc5, dc2tog) twice (12)
Rnd 33 (dc4, dc2tog) twice (10)
Rnd 34 (dc3, dc2tog) twice (8)
Rnd 35 (dc2, dc2tog) twice (6)
Rnd 36 (dc1, dc2tog) twice (4)
Stuff end lightly and sew flat across top
    to close.

LEGS (make two)
Working in Lime
Ch12 and sl st to join into a circle
Rnds 1–35 dc (35 rnds)
Rnd 36 (dc2tog) 6 times (6)
Stuff foot and sew flat across top to close.

PETALS (make six)
Working in Primrose
Ch20 and sl st to join into a circle
Rnd 1 (dc4, dc2 into next st) 4 times (24)
Rnd 2 (dc3, dc2 into next st) 6 times (30)
Rnd 3 (dc4, dc2 into next st) 6 times (36)
Rnds 4–6 dc (3 rnds)
Rnd 7 (dc10, dc2tog) 3 times (33)

Rnd 8 (dc9, dc2tog) 3 times (30)
Rnd 9 (dc8, dc2tog) 3 times (27)
Rnd 10 (dc7, dc2tog) 3 times (24)
Rnd 11 (dc6, dc2tog) 3 times (21)
Rnd 12 (dc5, dc2tog) 3 times (18)
Rnd 13 (dc4, dc2tog) 3 times (15)
Rnd 14 (dc3, dc2tog) 3 times (12)
Rnd 15 (dc2, dc2tog) 3 times (9)
Do not stuff, sew flat across top to close.

Make a ring of petals by dc along bottom of
    each petal with a ch4 in between each petal.
Sew into position on head (see pages 152–153).

TRUMPET
Working in Primrose
Ch42 and sl st to join into a circle
Rnds 1–3 dc (3 rnds)
Rnd 4 (dc5, dc2tog) 6 times (36)
Change to Yellow
Rnds 5–12 dc (8 rnds)
Rnd 13 (dc5, dc2 into next st) 6 times (42)
Rnd 14 (dc2 into next st) 42 times (84)
Rnd 15 (dc2 into next st) 84 times (168)
Sew into position.

Finish by sewing eyes into place with Black and
    Cream yarn.

Heather

A flower now very much associated with good luck, purple heather also symbolises admiration, while white heather offers protection and indicates that dreams will come true. The name heather is believed to come from the Scots word *haeddre*, which was used to describe a heathland, and the plant took on its association with luck from the Scottish legend of Malvina. In Scotland, it is still common to include a sprig of white heather in a bride's bouquet to bestow good fortune on the marriage, and long and happy lives for the bride and groom.

HEAD/BODY
Working in Green
Begin by dc6 into ring
Rnd 1 (dc2 into next st) 6 times (12 sts)
Rnd 2 (dc1, dc2 into next st) 6 times (18)
Rnd 3 (dc2, dc2 into next st) 6 times (24)
Rnd 4 (dc3, dc2 into next st) 6 times (30)
Rnd 5 (dc4, dc2 into next st) 6 times (36)
Rnd 6 (dc5, dc2 into next st) 6 times (42)
Rnds 7–19 dc (13 rnds)
Rnd 20 (dc5, dc2tog) 6 times (36)
Rnd 21 (dc4, dc2tog) 6 times (30)
Rnd 22 (dc3, dc2tog) 6 times (24)
Rnd 23 (dc2, dc2tog) 6 times (18)
Rnd 24 (dc2tog) 9 times (9)
Rnds 25–26 dc (2 rnds)
Rnd 27 (dc2 into next st) 9 times (18)
Rnd 28 (dc2, dc2 into next st) 6 times (24)
Rnds 29–34 dc (6 rnds)
Rnd 35 (dc3, dc2 into next st) 6 times (30)
Rnds 36–38 dc (3 rnds)
Rnd 39 (dc4, dc2 into next st) 6 times (36)
Rnd 40 dc12, (dc1, dc2 into next st) 6 times, dc12 (42)
Rnd 41 (dc6, dc2 into next st) 6 times (48)

Rnds 42–46 dc (5 rnds)
Rnd 47 (dc6, dc2tog) 6 times (42)
Rnd 48 (dc5, dc2tog) 6 times (36)
Rnd 49 dc
Rnd 50 (dc4, dc2tog) 6 times (30)
Rnd 51 (dc3, dc2tog) 6 times (24)
Rnd 52 (dc2, dc2tog) 6 times (18)
Rnd 53 (dc2tog) 9 times (9)

ARMS/LEGS (make four)
Working in Green
Ch12 and sl st to join into a circle
Rnds 1–35 dc (35 rnds)
Rnd 36 (dc2tog) 6 times (6)
Stuff end and sew flat across top to close.

FRONDS (make four)
Working in Green
Begin by dc6 into ring
Rnd 1 (dc2 into next st) 6 times (12)
Rnds 2–12 dc (11 rnds)
Sew flat across top to close.
Sew two fronds into position diagonally on each arm.
Continues overleaf

MADE IN Green and Magenta
YARN QUANTITIES 75g foliage, 50g flowers
TIME TO GROW Slow grower
COLOUR VARIANTS Pink, Magenta, Amethyst, Cream, Peony
REQUIRES Just the basics!

PETALS (make 31)

Working in Magenta
Begin by dc6 into ring
Rnd 1 (dc2 into next st) 6 times (12)
Rnds 2–4 dc (3 rnds)
Rnd 5 (dc2, dc2tog) 3 times (9)
Rnd 6 (dc1, dc2tog) 3 times (6)
Break yarn and sew in ends but do not gather
    sts. This leaves a hole at end of petal.

Work six vertical lines of five petals onto head
    as follows:

Working in Green
Sl st through starting ring of petal and into head
    at neck, *ch3, sl st into head approximately
    5 rnds up, sl st into next petal and repeat
    from * to create a line of five petals.

Repeat five more times around head, then sew
    final petal into position on top of head.

Finish by sewing eyes into place with Black and
    Cream yarn.

Iris

Iris was the goddess of the rainbow in Greek mythology, and many believe that the flower is named after her. She carried messages from heaven to earth on the arc of the rainbow, and was a companion to female souls on the way to heaven. To this day, it is still a tradition in some cultures to plant purple irises on women's graves so that Iris will guide them up to heaven. Irises can represent faith, hope, courage, wisdom and admiration and, with over 200 species and lots of variants, specific colours attach further meanings to their pretty blooms. Purple irises bring a message of wisdom and compliments, while a bouquet of blue irises promises hope and faith. Yellow irises symbolise passion, while white irises symbolise purity.

HEAD/BODY
Working in Yellow
Begin by dc6 into ring
Rnd 1 (dc2 into next st) 6 times (12 sts)
Rnd 2 (dc1, dc2 into next st) 6 times (18)
Rnd 3 (dc2, dc2 into next st) 6 times (24)
Rnd 4 (dc3, dc2 into next st) 6 times (30)
Rnd 5 (dc4, dc2 into next st) 6 times (36)
Rnd 6 (dc5, dc2 into next st) 6 times (42)
Rnd 7 (dc6, dc2 into next st) 6 times (48)
Rnd 8 (dc7, dc2 into next st) 6 times (54)
Rnds 9–13 dc (5 rnds)
Rnd 14 (dc7, dc2tog) 6 times (48)
Rnd 15 (dc6, dc2tog) 6 times (42)
Rnd 16 (dc5, dc2tog) 6 times (36)
Rnd 17 (dc4, dc2tog) 6 times (30)
Rnd 18 (dc3, dc2tog) 6 times (24)
Rnd 19 (dc2, dc2tog) 6 times (18)
Rnd 20 (dc2tog) 9 times (9)
Change to Lime
Rnds 21–22 dc (2 rnds)

Rnd 23 (dc2 into next st) 9 times (18)
Rnd 24 (dc2, dc2 into next st) 6 times (24)
Rnds 25–30 dc (6 rnds)
Rnd 31 (dc3, dc2 into next st) 6 times (30)
Rnds 32–34 dc (3 rnds)
Rnd 35 (dc4, dc2 into next st) 6 times (36)
Rnd 36 dc12, (dc1, dc2 into next st) 6 times, dc12 (42)
Rnd 37 (dc6, dc2 into next st) 6 times (48)
Rnds 38–42 dc (5 rnds)
Rnd 43 (dc6, dc2tog) 6 times (42)
Rnd 44 (dc5, dc2tog) 6 times (36)
Rnd 45 dc
Rnd 46 (dc4, dc2tog) 6 times (30)
Rnd 47 (dc3, dc2tog) 6 times (24)
Rnd 48 (dc2, dc2tog) 6 times (18)
Rnd 49 (dc2tog) 9 times (9)

ARMS (make two)
Working in Lime
Continues overleaf

MADE IN Lime, Amethyst and Yellow (overleaf with Blue flower)
YARN QUANTITIES 50g foliage, 50g flower, 25g flower contrast
TIME TO GROW Moderate
COLOUR VARIANTS Amethyst, Cream, Violet, Hyacinth
REQUIRES htr, tr

Ch12 and sl st to join into a circle
Rnds 1–20 dc (20 rnds)
Rnd 21 (dc5, dc2 into next st) twice (14)
Rnd 22 (dc6, dc2 into next st) twice (16)
Rnd 23 (dc7, dc2 into next st) twice (18)
Rnds 24–29 dc (6 rnds)
Rnd 30 (dc7, dc2tog) twice (16)
Rnd 31 (dc6, dc2tog) twice (14)
Rnd 32 (dc5, dc2tog) twice (12)
Rnd 33 (dc4, dc2tog) twice (10)
Rnd 34 (dc3, dc2tog) twice (8)
Rnd 35 (dc2, dc2tog) twice (6)
Rnd 36 (dc1, dc2tog) twice (4)
Stuff end lightly and sew flat across top
   to close.

LEGS (make two)
Working in Lime
Ch12 and sl st to join into a circle
Rnds 1–35 dc (35 rnds)
Rnd 36 (dc2tog) 6 times (6)
Stuff foot and sew flat across top to close.

PETALS (make three)
Working in Amethyst
Begin by dc6 into ring
Rnd 1 (dc2 into next st) 6 times (12)
Rnd 2 (dc1, dc2 into next st) 6 times (18)
Rnd 3 (dc2, dc2 into next st) 6 times (24)
Rnd 4 (dc3, dc2 into next st) 6 times (30)
Rnd 5 (dc4, dc2 into next st) 6 times (36)
Rnds 6–10 dc (5 rnds)

Rnd 11 (dc2tog, dc4) 6 times (30)
Rnd 12 (dc2tog, dc3) 6 times (24)
Rnds 13–17 dc (5 rnds)
Rnd 18 (dc3, dc2 into next st) 6 times (30)
Rnds 19–20 dc (2 rnds)
Rnd 21 (dc4, dc2 into next st) 6 times (36)
Sew flat across top to close.

Make a ring of petals by dc along bottom of
   each petal.
Sew into position on head (see pages 152–153).

CENTRES (make three; see chart)
Working in Yellow
Ch10, turn and work back down chain
   as follows:
dc3, htr3, tr3
Sew into position on top of petals.

Sew petals into position on head.

Finish by sewing eyes into place with Black and
   Cream yarn.

Hyacinth

This bloom is dedicated to the Greek sun god Apollo (also known for archery, truth and prophecy), and in Victorian times these flowers signified games, sports and play. With this in mind you could make this flower for someone who loves to play sports as a form of encouragement for an upcoming game – maybe even in the colours of their team. This Spring flower, also known as a symbol of peace, commitment and sincerity, has historically been associated with sorrow for wrongs committed. As a result, making a purple or blue hyacinth as a gift for someone asks for forgiveness when you have behaved thoughtlessly, whereas white hyacinths are associated with prayers and hope.

HEAD/BODY
Working in Hyacinth
Begin by dc6 into ring
Rnd 1 (dc2 into next st) 6 times (12 sts)
Rnd 2 (dc1, dc2 into next st) 6 times (18)
Rnd 3 (dc2, dc2 into next st) 6 times (24)
Rnd 4 (dc3, dc2 into next st) 6 times (30)
Rnd 5 (dc4, dc2 into next st) 6 times (36)
Rnd 6 (dc5, dc2 into next st) 6 times (42)
Rnds 7–19 dc (13 rnds)
Rnd 20 (dc5, dc2tog) 6 times (36)
Rnd 21 (dc4, dc2tog) 6 times (30)
Rnd 22 (dc3, dc2tog) 6 times (24)
Rnd 23 (dc2, dc2tog) 6 times (18)
Rnd 24 (dc2tog) 9 times (9)
Change to Lime
Rnds 25–26 dc (2 rnds)
Rnd 27 (dc2 into next st) 9 times (18)
Rnd 28 (dc2, dc2 into next st) 6 times (24)
Rnds 29–34 dc (6 rnds)
Rnd 35 (dc3, dc2 into next st) 6 times (30)
Rnds 36–38 dc (3 rnds)

Rnd 39 (dc4, dc2 into next st) 6 times (36)
Rnd 40 dc12, (dc1, dc2 into next st) 6 times, dc12 (42)
Rnd 41 (dc6, dc2 into next st) 6 times (48)
Rnds 42–46 dc (5 rnds)
Rnd 47 (dc6, dc2tog) 6 times (42)
Rnd 48 (dc5, dc2tog) 6 times (36)
Rnd 49 dc
Rnd 50 (dc4, dc2tog) 6 times (30)
Rnd 51 (dc3, dc2tog) 6 times (24)
Rnd 52 (dc2, dc2tog) 6 times (18)
Rnd 53 (dc2tog) 9 times (9)

ARMS (make two)
Working in Lime
Ch12 and sl st to join into a circle
Rnds 1–20 dc (20 rnds)
Rnd 21 (dc5, dc2 into next st) twice (14)
Rnd 22 (dc6, dc2 into next st) twice (16)
Rnd 23 (dc7, dc2 into next st) twice (18)
Rnds 24–29 dc (6 rnds)
Continues overleaf

MADE IN Lime and Hyacinth
YARN QUANTITIES 50g foliage, 50g flower
TIME TO GROW Moderate
COLOUR VARIANTS Primrose, Coral, Violet, Peony, Sage, Pink, Cream
REQUIRES htr, tr

Rnd 30 (dc7, dc2tog) twice (16)
Rnd 31 (dc6, dc2tog) twice (14)
Rnd 32 (dc5, dc2tog) twice (12)
Rnd 33 (dc4, dc2tog) twice (10)
Rnd 34 (dc3, dc2tog) twice (8)
Rnd 35 (dc2, dc2tog) twice (6)
Rnd 36 (dc1, dc2tog) twice (4)
Stuff end lightly and sew flat across top to close.

LEGS (make two)
Working in Lime
Ch12 and sl st to join into a circle
Rnds 1–35 dc (35 rnds)
Rnd 36 (dc2tog) 6 times (6)
Stuff foot and sew flat across top to close.

FLOWERS (make 25; see chart)
Working in Hyacinth
Ch6 and sl st to join into a circle
Rnd 1 dc
*ch6, turn and work back down chain as follows:
sl st1, dc1, htr2, miss 1, miss 1 st along base, sl st1
Repeat from * twice more.

Sl st into missed stitch from previous rnd
*ch6, turn and work back down chain
    as follows:

sl st1, dc1, htr2, miss 1, sl st1 into missed stitch in
    middle of next petal
Repeat from * twice more.
Break yarn.

Sew flowers into position by sewing six vertical
    lines of four flowers around head.
Sew final flower into position on centre top
    of head.

Finish by sewing eyes into place with Black and
    Cream yarn.

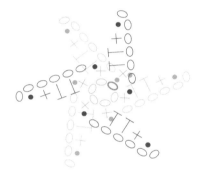

Tulip

Like many other flowers, tulips have strong associations attached to them, but one of the most common meanings is deep and perfect love. As with other Spring flowers, tulips also mean rebirth and starting afresh, making them a perfect gift for anyone who has just moved into a new home or started a new job. The Victorians also associated tulips with a sense of charity and working together to achieve a sense of greater good, so they make a brilliant gift for a team or colleague. There are over 150 species of tulip, with over 3000 different varieties, and they have now been cultivated in every colour except deep blue.

HEAD/BODY
Working in Violet
Begin by dc6 into ring
Rnd 1 (dc2 into next st) 6 times (12 sts)
Rnd 2 (dc1, dc2 into next st) 6 times (18)
Rnd 3 (dc2, dc2 into next st) 6 times (24)
Rnd 4 (dc3, dc2 into next st) 6 times (30)
Rnd 5 (dc4, dc2 into next st) 6 times (36)
Rnd 6 (dc5, dc2 into next st) 6 times (42)
Rnd 7 (dc6, dc2 into next st) 6 times (48)
Rnd 8 (dc7, dc2 into next st) 6 times (54)
Rnds 9–13 dc (5 rnds)
Rnd 14 (dc7, dc2tog) 6 times (48)
Rnd 15 (dc6, dc2tog) 6 times (42)
Rnd 16 (dc5, dc2tog) 6 times (36)
Rnd 17 (dc4, dc2tog) 6 times (30)
Rnd 18 (dc3, dc2tog) 6 times (24)
Rnd 19 (dc2, dc2tog) 6 times (18)
Rnd 20 (dc2tog) 9 times (9)
Change to Lime
Rnds 21–22 dc (2 rnds)
Rnd 23 (dc2 into next st) 9 times (18)
Rnd 24 (dc2, dc2 into next st) 6 times (24)

Rnds 25–30 dc (6 rnds)
Rnd 31 (dc3, dc2 into next st) 6 times (30)
Rnds 32–34 dc (3 rnds)
Rnd 35 (dc4, dc2 into next st) 6 times (36)
Rnd 36 dc12, (dc1, dc2 into next st) 6 times, dc12 (42)
Rnd 37 (dc6, dc2 into next st) 6 times (48)
Rnds 38–42 dc (5 rnds)
Rnd 43 (dc6, dc2tog) 6 times (42)
Rnd 44 (dc5, dc2tog) 6 times (36)
Rnd 45 dc
Rnd 46 (dc4, dc2tog) 6 times (30)
Rnd 47 (dc3, dc2tog) 6 times (24)
Rnd 48 (dc2, dc2tog) 6 times (18)
Rnd 49 (dc2tog) 9 times (9)

ARMS (make two)
Working in Lime
Ch12 and sl st to join into a circle
Rnds 1–20 dc (20 rnds)
Rnd 21 (dc5, dc2 into next st) twice (14)
Rnd 22 (dc6, dc2 into next st) twice (16)
Continues overleaf

MADE IN Lime and Violet (overleaf with flowers in Pink and Peony, and Amethyst and Violet)
YARN QUANTITIES 50g foliage, 50g flower, 25g flower contrast
TIME TO GROW Moderate
COLOUR VARIANTS Pink, Magenta, Amethyst, Cream, Yellow, Primrose, Violet, Ruby
REQUIRES htr, tr, dtr

Rnd 23 (dc7, dc2 into next st) twice (18)
Rnds 24–29 dc (6 rnds)
Rnd 30 (dc7, dc2tog) twice (16)
Rnd 31 (dc6, dc2tog) twice (14)
Rnd 32 (dc5, dc2tog) twice (12)
Rnd 33 (dc4, dc2tog) twice (10)
Rnd 34 (dc3, dc2tog) twice (8)
Rnd 35 (dc2, dc2tog) twice (6)
Rnd 36 (dc1, dc2tog) twice (4)
Stuff end lightly and sew flat across top to close.

LEGS (make two)
Working in Lime
Ch12 and sl st to join into a circle
Rnds 1–35 dc (35 rnds)
Rnd 36 (dc2tog) 6 times (6)
Stuff foot and sew flat across top to close.

PETALS (make three)
Working in Violet
Begin by dc6 into ring
Rnd 1 (dc2 into next st) 6 times (12)
Rnd 2 (dc1, dc2 into next st) 6 times (18)
Rnd 3 (dc2, dc2 into next st) 6 times (24)
Rnd 4 (dc3, dc2 into next st) 6 times (30)
Rnds 5–7 dc (3 rnds)
Rnd 8 (dc4, dc2 into next st) 6 times (36)
Rnd 9 dc

Rnd 10 (dc5, dc2 into next st) 6 times (42)
Rnds 11–13 dc (3 rnds)
Rnd 14 (dc5, dc2tog) 6 times (36)
Rnd 15 (dc4, dc2tog) 6 times (30)
Rnds 16–18 dc (3 rnds)
Rnd 19 (dc2tog, dc8) 3 times (27)
Rnd 20 dc
Rnd 21 (dc2tog, dc7) 3 times (24)
Rnd 22 (dc2tog, dc6) 3 times (21)
Rnd 23 (dc2tog, dc5) 3 times (18)
Rnd 24 (dc2tog) 9 times (9)
Break yarn, gather sts and sew in end.

PETAL EDGE AND CENTRE
To make variegated flowers, work this detail in
   a contrasting yarn as shown on this page.
Rejoin to one side of bottom of petal and
   dc two rnds around edge. Do not break
   yarn. Ch16, sl st into centre of petal
   approximately 6 rnds down from top
   and work back down chain as follows:
sl st3, dc3, htr3, tr3, dtr3

Sew petals into position around head.

Finish by sewing eyes into place with Black and
   Cream yarn.

Lily

Lilies have many meanings, but the most common historical associations are with purity and fertility. The simple beauty of the lily has also given it symbolism associated with femininity, love and grief, dating back to Ancient Egyptian times. Lilies are popular at both weddings and funerals, managing to embody the purity of a new relationship and to symbolise the restoration of innocence after death. This is a flower that offers comfort to us at some of our happiest and saddest moments.

HEAD/BODY
Working in Cream
Begin by dc6 into ring
Rnd 1 (dc2 into next st) 6 times (12 sts)
Rnd 2 (dc1, dc2 into next st) 6 times (18)
Rnd 3 (dc2, dc2 into next st) 6 times (24)
Rnd 4 (dc3, dc2 into next st) 6 times (30)
Rnd 5 (dc4, dc2 into next st) 6 times (36)
Rnd 6 (dc5, dc2 into next st) 6 times (42)
Rnd 7 (dc6, dc2 into next st) 6 times (48)
Rnd 8 (dc7, dc2 into next st) 6 times (54)
Rnds 9–13 dc (5 rnds)
Rnd 14 (dc7, dc2tog) 6 times (48)
Rnd 15 (dc6, dc2tog) 6 times (42)
Rnd 16 (dc5, dc2tog) 6 times (36)
Rnd 17 (dc4, dc2tog) 6 times (30)
Rnd 18 (dc3, dc2tog) 6 times (24)
Rnd 19 (dc2, dc2tog) 6 times (18)
Rnd 20 (dc2tog) 9 times (9)
Change to Lime
Rnds 21–22 dc (2 rnds)
Rnd 23 (dc2 into next st) 9 times (18)
Rnd 24 (dc2, dc2 into next st) 6 times (24)
Rnds 25–30 dc (6 rnds)

Rnd 31 (dc3, dc2 into next st) 6 times (30)
Rnds 32–34 dc (3 rnds)
Rnd 35 (dc4, dc2 into next st) 6 times (36)
Rnd 36 dc12, (dc1, dc2 into next st) 6 times, dc12 (42)
Rnd 37 (dc6, dc2 into next st) 6 times (48)
Rnds 38–42 dc (5 rnds)
Rnd 43 (dc6, dc2tog) 6 times (42)
Rnd 44 (dc5, dc2tog) 6 times (36)
Rnd 45 dc
Rnd 46 (dc4, dc2tog) 6 times (30)
Rnd 47 (dc3, dc2tog) 6 times (24)
Rnd 48 (dc2, dc2tog) 6 times (18)
Rnd 49 (dc2tog) 9 times (9)

ARMS (make two)
Working in Lime
Ch12 and sl st to join into a circle
Rnds 1–20 dc (20 rnds)
Rnd 21 (dc5, dc2 into next st) twice (14)
Rnd 22 (dc6, dc2 into next st) twice (16)
Rnd 23 (dc7, dc2 into next st) twice (18)
Rnds 24–29 dc (6 rnds)
Continues overleaf

MADE IN Lime, Cream and Fudge
YARN QUANTITIES 50g foliage, 100g flower, 25g stamens
TIME TO GROW Slow grower
COLOUR VARIANTS Pink, Magenta, Amethyst, Cream, Peony, Ruby, Yellow, Orange
REQUIRES Slip stitch chain

Rnd 30 (dc7, dc2tog) twice (16)
Rnd 31 (dc6, dc2tog) twice (14)
Rnd 32 (dc5, dc2tog) twice (12)
Rnd 33 (dc4, dc2tog) twice (10)
Rnd 34 (dc3, dc2tog) twice (8)
Rnd 35 (dc2, dc2tog) twice (6)
Rnd 36 (dc1, dc2tog) twice (4)
Stuff end lightly and sew flat across top to close.

LEGS (make two)
Working in Lime
Ch12 and sl st to join into a circle
Rnds 1–35 dc (35 rnds)
Rnd 36 (dc2tog) 6 times (6)
Stuff foot and sew flat across top to close.

PETALS (make six)
Working in Cream
Ch18 and sl st to join into a circle
Rnd 1 dc
Rnd 2 (dc2, dc2 into next st) 6 times (24)
Rnd 3 dc
Rnd 4 (dc3, dc2 into next st) 6 times (30)
Rnds 5–9 dc (5 rnds)
Rnd 10 (dc8, dc2tog) 3 times (27)
Rnds 11–15 dc (5 rnds)
Rnd 16 (dc7, dc2tog) 3 times (24)
Rnds 17–19 dc (3 rnds)
Rnd 20 (dc6, dc2tog) 3 times (21)

Rnds 21–22 dc (2 rnds)
Rnd 23 (dc5, dc2tog) 3 times (18)
Rnd 24 dc
Rnd 25 (dc1, dc2tog) 6 times (12)
Rnd 26 (dc2, dc2tog) 3 times (9)
Rnd 27 (dc1, dc2tog) 3 times (6)

Make two rings of petals by dc along
    bottom of each petal with a ch5 in
    between each petal.
Sew into position on head (see pages 152–153).

STAMEN FILAMENT
Working in Lime
Sl st into position on top of head
Work three ch12 and one ch18 SLIP STITCH
    CHAINS (see page 154).

STAMEN ANTHER
Working in Fudge
Sl st into position on end of STAMEN
    FILAMENT
(ch3, turn and dc2 back down ch, sl st into
    base) twice
Break yarn and repeat for the other three.

Finish by sewing eyes into place with Black and
    Cream yarn.

Allium

One of my personal favourites for growing in my flowerbeds and vegetable patch alike, these bold plants grow from a bulb that sends up a single stem, blooming into a perfect sphere of tiny flowers. The allium is associated with good fortune, patience and grace and is the perfect flower to gift someone to bring them good luck. The *Allium* genus includes hundreds of species of more commonly known flowering plants, including culinary varieties like garlic, chives, onions and shallots, so this flower is also the perfect gift for any foodie.

HEAD/BODY
Working in Amethyst
Begin by dc6 into ring
Rnd 1 (dc2 into next st) 6 times (12 sts)
Rnd 2 (dc1, dc2 into next st) 6 times (18)
Rnd 3 (dc2, dc2 into next st) 6 times (24)
Rnd 4 (dc3, dc2 into next st) 6 times (30)
Rnd 5 (dc4, dc2 into next st) 6 times (36)
Rnd 6 (dc5, dc2 into next st) 6 times (42)
Rnd 7 (dc6, dc2 into next st) 6 times (48)
Rnd 8 (dc7, dc2 into next st) 6 times (54)
Rnds 9–16 dc (8 rnds)
Rnd 17 (dc7, dc2tog) 6 times (48)
Rnd 18 (dc6, dc2tog) 6 times (42)
Rnd 19 (dc5, dc2tog) 6 times (36)
Rnd 20 (dc4, dc2tog) 6 times (30)
Rnd 21 (dc3, dc2tog) 6 times (24)
Rnd 22 (dc2, dc2tog) 6 times (18)
Rnd 23 (dc2tog) 9 times (9)
Change to Green
Rnds 24–25 dc (2 rnds)
Rnd 26 (dc2 into next st) 9 times (18)
Rnd 27 (dc2, dc2 into next st) 6 times (24)
Rnds 28–33 dc (6 rnds)

Rnd 34 (dc3, dc2 into next st) 6 times (30)
Rnds 35–37 dc (3 rnds)
Rnd 38 (dc4, dc2 into next st) 6 times (36)
Rnd 39 dc12, (dc1, dc2 into next st) 6 times, dc12 (42)
Rnd 40 (dc6, dc2 into next st) 6 times (48)
Rnds 41–45 dc (5 rnds)
Rnd 46 (dc6, dc2tog) 6 times (42)
Rnd 47 (dc5, dc2tog) 6 times (36)
Rnd 48 dc
Rnd 49 (dc4, dc2tog) 6 times (30)
Rnd 50 (dc3, dc2tog) 6 times (24)
Rnd 51 (dc2, dc2tog) 6 times (18)
Rnd 52 (dc2tog) 9 times (9)

ARMS (make two)
Working in Green
Ch12 and sl st to join into a circle
Rnds 1–20 dc (20 rnds)
Rnd 21 (dc5, dc2 into next st) twice (14)
Rnd 22 (dc6, dc2 into next st) twice (16)
Rnd 23 (dc7, dc2 into next st) twice (18)
Rnds 24–29 dc (6 rnds)
Continues overleaf

MADE IN Green, Amethyst and Lime (overleaf with Violet flowers)
YARN QUANTITIES 50g foliage, 50g flower, 25g flower contrast
TIME TO GROW Moderate
COLOUR VARIANTS Pink, Amethyst, Cream, Hyacinth
REQUIRES htr, tr, slip stitch chain

Rnd 30 (dc7, dc2tog) twice (16)
Rnd 31 (dc6, dc2tog) twice (14)
Rnd 32 (dc5, dc2tog) twice (12)
Rnd 33 (dc4, dc2tog) twice (10)
Rnd 34 (dc3, dc2tog) twice (8)
Rnd 35 (dc2, dc2tog) twice (6)
Rnd 36 (dc1, dc2tog) twice (4)
Stuff end lightly and sew flat across top to close.

LEGS (make two)
Working in Green
Ch12 and sl st to join into a circle
Rnds 1–35 dc (35 rnds)
Rnd 36 (dc2tog) 6 times (6)
Stuff foot and sew flat across top to close.

FLOWERS (make approximately 25; see chart)
Working in Amethyst
Begin by dc6 into ring
Work six ch4 SLIP STITCH CHAINS (see page 154) around edge.
Break yarn.

Sew flowers into position to cover head.

FLOWER CENTRES (make approximately 25)
Working in Lime
Work directly onto centre of flowers as follows:
sl st into position in centre of flower, ch2, turn and dc3 into first ch.
Break yarn and gather all sts, then sew ends through.

Finish by sewing eyes into place with Black and Cream yarn.

Ranunculus

These flowers generally symbolise charm and attraction, regardless of their colour, and as they offer a full spectrum of colours, they work well as a gift for every kind of special occasion. Give your ranunculus an extra layer of meaning with your choice of colour: from orange blooms to symbolise positive energy, joy and happiness, to reds and pinks for romance, through to purples for mystery. This flower has a very beautiful structure, made even more attractive by such a bold range of hues.

HEAD/BODY
Working in Orange
Begin by dc6 into ring
Rnd 1 (dc2 into next st) 6 times (12 sts)
Rnd 2 (dc1, dc2 into next st) 6 times (18)
Rnd 3 (dc2, dc2 into next st) 6 times (24)
Rnd 4 (dc3, dc2 into next st) 6 times (30)
Rnd 5 (dc4, dc2 into next st) 6 times (36)
Rnd 6 (dc5, dc2 into next st) 6 times (42)
Rnd 7 (dc6, dc2 into next st) 6 times (48)
Rnd 8 (dc7, dc2 into next st) 6 times (54)
Rnds 9–13 dc (5 rnds)
Rnd 14 (dc7, dc2tog) 6 times (48)
Rnd 15 (dc6, dc2tog) 6 times (42)
Rnd 16 (dc5, dc2tog) 6 times (36)
Rnd 17 (dc4, dc2tog) 6 times (30)
Rnd 18 (dc3, dc2tog) 6 times (24)
Rnd 19 (dc2, dc2tog) 6 times (18)
Rnd 20 (dc2tog) 9 times (9)
Change to Lime
Rnds 21–22 dc (2 rnds)
Rnd 23 (dc2 into next st) 9 times (18)
Rnd 24 (dc2, dc2 into next st) 6 times (24)
Rnds 25–30 dc (6 rnds)

Rnd 31 (dc3, dc2 into next st) 6 times (30)
Rnds 32–34 dc (3 rnds)
Rnd 35 (dc4, dc2 into next st) 6 times (36)
Rnd 36 dc12, (dc1, dc2 into next st) 6 times, dc12 (42)
Rnd 37 (dc6, dc2 into next st) 6 times (48)
Rnds 38–42 dc (5 rnds)
Rnd 43 (dc6, dc2tog) 6 times (42)
Rnd 44 (dc5, dc2tog) 6 times (36)
Rnd 45 dc
Rnd 46 (dc4, dc2tog) 6 times (30)
Rnd 47 (dc3, dc2tog) 6 times (24)
Rnd 48 (dc2, dc2tog) 6 times (18)
Rnd 49 (dc2tog) 9 times (9)

ARMS (make two)
Working in Lime
Ch12 and sl st to join into a circle
Rnds 1–15 dc (15 rnds)
Rnd 16 (dc1, dc2 into next st) 6 times (18)
Rnd 17 (dc2, dc2 into next st) 6 times (24)
Count 8 sts back, split these sts into an 8 st rnd and work as follows:
Continues overleaf

MADE IN Lime and Orange
YARN QUANTITIES 50g foliage, 50g flower
TIME TO GROW Speedy grower
COLOUR VARIANTS Pink, Magenta, Cream, Peony, Coral, Primrose, Yellow
REQUIRES tr, dtr, ttr, qtr, splitting the round (see illustration 2, page 33)

Rnd 1 dc
Rnd 2 (dc1, dc2 into next st) 4 times (12)

Dc3, count back 6 sts, split these 6 sts and dc3.
Work this 6-st rnd as follows:
Rnds 1–2 dc (2 rnds)
Rnd 3 (dc1, dc2tog) twice (4)
Break yarn.
Rejoin on remaining 6 sts and work as follows:
Rnd 1 dc
Rnd 2 (dc1, dc2tog) twice (4)
Break yarn.

Miss 4 sts along main stem, rejoin and dc8, split
    these sts into an 8-st round and work as follows:
Rnd 1 (dc1, dc2 into next st) 4 times (12)

Dc3, count back 6 sts, split these 6 sts and dc3.
Work this 6-st rnd as follows:
Rnds 1–2 dc (2 rnds)
Rnd 3 (dc1, dc2tog) twice (4)
Break yarn.
Rejoin on remaining 6 sts and work as follows:
Rnd 1 dc
Rnd 2 (dc1, dc2tog) twice (4)
Break yarn.

Rejoin and work central 8-st round as follows
    (4 sts from each side):
Rnds 1–6 dc (6 rnds)
Rnd 7 (dc1, dc2 into next st) 4 times (12)
Rnd 8 (dc1, dc2 into next st) 6 times (18)

Dc3, count back 6 sts, split these sts into a 6-st
    round and work as follows:
Rnd 1 dc
Rnd 2 (dc1, dc2tog) twice (4)
Break yarn.
Miss 3 central sts, dc6, split these sts into a 6-st
    round and work as follows:
Rnd 1 dc
Rnd 2 (dc1, dc2tog) twice (4)
Break yarn.
Rejoin and work central 6-st round as follows
    (3 sts from each side):
Rnd 1–3 dc (3 rnds)

Rnd 4 (dc1, dc2tog) twice (4)
Break yarn.
Stuff end lightly and sew flat across top to close.

LEGS (make two)
Working in Lime
Ch12 and sl st to join into a circle
Rnds 1–35 dc (35 rnds)
Rnd 36 (dc2tog) 6 times (6)
Stuff foot and sew flat across top to close.

PETALS
Working in Orange
Sl st into position at centre front of neck on
    colour change line.
Ch3 and work a rnd of tr around face, working
    directly into head sts. Sl st back into first st at
    neck to join into a circle. Break yarn.

Sl st into position at centre back of neck on
    colour change line and work a rnd of dtr
    behind previous rnd. Sl st into first st to join
    into a circle. Break yarn.

Sl st into position behind previous rnd, ch4
    and work another rnd of dtr behind previous
    rnd. Sl st into first st to join into a circle.
    Break yarn.

Sl st into position behind previous rnd, ch5
    and work another rnd of ttr behind previous
    rnd. Sl st into first st to join into a circle.
    Break yarn.

Sl st into position behind previous rnd, ch6
    and work another rnd of qtr behind previous
    rnd. Sl st into first st to join into a circle.
    Break yarn.

Turn so that back of head is facing you and
    work two rnds of qtr. Sl st into first st to join
    into a circle.

Finish by sewing eyes into place with Black and
    Cream yarn.

Carnation

A pretty flower with lots of different meanings across the world, the carnation can sometimes be overlooked as the understudy in a bouquet rather than the star – but it should not be left off your making list. It is the flower traditionally connected with the first wedding anniversary, and has associations with young secret admirers. Send a message of admiration with a crocheted carnation, but pick your yarn colour carefully. While white means sweet and lovely, and pink carnations are associated with female love and a mother's unconditional love, yellow carnations can signify disdain and rejection. However, give a single flower in one solid colour and it means 'yes'.

HEAD/BODY

Working in Cream
Begin by dc6 into ring
Rnd 1 (dc2 into next st) 6 times (12 sts)
Rnd 2 (dc1, dc2 into next st) 6 times (18)
Rnd 3 (dc2, dc2 into next st) 6 times (24)
Rnd 4 (dc3, dc2 into next st) 6 times (30)
Rnd 5 (dc4, dc2 into next st) 6 times (36)
Rnd 6 (dc5, dc2 into next st) 6 times (42)
Rnd 7 (dc6, dc2 into next st) 6 times (48)
Rnd 8 (dc7, dc2 into next st) 6 times (54)
Rnds 9–13 dc (5 rnds)
Rnd 14 (dc7, dc2tog) 6 times (48)
Rnd 15 (dc6, dc2tog) 6 times (42)
Rnd 16 (dc5, dc2tog) 6 times (36)
Rnd 17 (dc4, dc2tog) 6 times (30)
Rnd 18 (dc3, dc2tog) 6 times (24)
Rnd 19 (dc2, dc2tog) 6 times (18)
Rnd 20 (dc2tog) 9 times (9)
Change to Lime
Rnds 21–22 dc (2 rnds)
Rnd 23 (dc2 into next st) 9 times (18)

Rnd 24 (dc2, dc2 into next st) 6 times (24)
Rnds 25–30 dc (6 rnds)
Rnd 31 (dc3, dc2 into next st) 6 times (30)
Rnds 32–34 dc (3 rnds)
Rnd 35 (dc4, dc2 into next st) 6 times (36)
Rnd 36 dc12, (dc1, dc2 into next st) 6 times, dc12 (42)
Rnd 37 (dc6, dc2 into next st) 6 times (48)
Rnds 38–42 dc (5 rnds)
Rnd 43 (dc6, dc2tog) 6 times (42)
Rnd 44 (dc5, dc2tog) 6 times (36)
Rnd 45 dc
Rnd 46 (dc4, dc2tog) 6 times (30)
Rnd 47 (dc3, dc2tog) 6 times (24)
Rnd 48 (dc2, dc2tog) 6 times (18)
Rnd 49 (dc2tog) 9 times (9)

ARMS (make two)

Working in Lime
Ch12 and sl st to join into a circle
Rnds 1–20 dc (20 rnds)
Continues overleaf

MADE IN Lime, Cream and Magenta (overleaf with Pink and Peony flower)
YARN QUANTITIES 75g foliage, 50g flower, 25g flower contrast
TIME TO GROW Slow grower
COLOUR VARIANTS Pink, Magenta, Amethyst, Cream, Peony
REQUIRES htr, tr

Rnd 21 (dc5, dc2 into next st) twice (14)
Rnd 22 (dc6, dc2 into next st) twice (16)
Rnd 23 (dc7, dc2 into next st) twice (18)
Rnds 24–29 dc (6 rnds)
Rnd 30 (dc7, dc2tog) twice (16)
Rnd 31 (dc6, dc2tog) twice (14)
Rnd 32 (dc5, dc2tog) twice (12)
Rnd 33 (dc4, dc2tog) twice (10)
Rnd 34 (dc3, dc2tog) twice (8)
Rnd 35 (dc2, dc2tog) twice (6)
Rnd 36 (dc1, dc2tog) twice (4)
Stuff end lightly and sew flat across top to close.

LEGS (make two)
Working in Lime
Ch12 and sl st to join into a circle
Rnds 1–35 dc (35 rnds)
Rnd 36 (dc2tog) 6 times (6)
Stuff foot and sew flat across top to close.

PETALS (make nine)
Working in Cream
Begin by dc6 into ring
Rnd 1 (dc2 into next st) 6 times (12)
Rnd 2 (dc1, dc2 into next st) 6 times (18)
Rnd 3 (dc2, dc2 into next st) 6 times (24)

Rnd 4 (dc2 into next st) 12 times, (dc3, dc2 into next st) 3 times (39)
Rnd 5 (dc2 into next st) 24 times, (dc4, dc2 into next st) 3 times (66)
Rnd 6 dc48 Magenta, (dc5, dc2 into next st) 3 times Cream (69)

COLLAR
Working in Lime
Ch15 and sl st to join into a circle
Rnd 1 (dc4, dc2 into next st) 3 times (18)
Rnd 2 (dc2, dc2 into next st) 6 times (24)
Rnd 3 (dc3, dc2 into next st) 6 times (30)
Rnd 4 (dc4, dc2 into next st) 6 times (36)
Rnd 5 dc
Rnd 6 (dc3, htr1, tr1, htr1) 6 times
Break yarn.

Add collar before stuffing (see page 155).

Sew petals into position on head with three petals around centre top and remaining petals overlapping around bottom of head.

Finish by sewing eyes into place with Black and Cream yarn.

Bluebell

One of the prettiest and most popular flowers, found in gardens and woods alike, these bell-shaped blooms are embedded in folklore. They are called 'fairy flowers', as the fairies are said to have rung the little blue bells to summon their kin. Others believed that wearing a wreath made of bluebells made you able to speak only the truth. For the Romantic poets, the bluebell represented regret and solitude, but in the language of flowers more generally, they represent everlasting love, constancy and humility.

HEAD/BODY
Working in Violet
Begin by dc6 into ring
Rnd 1 (dc2 into next st) 6 times (12 sts)
Rnd 2 (dc1, dc2 into next st) 6 times (18)
Rnd 3 (dc2, dc2 into next st) 6 times (24)
Rnd 4 (dc3, dc2 into next st) 6 times (30)
Rnd 5 (dc4, dc2 into next st) 6 times (36)
Rnd 6 (dc5, dc2 into next st) 6 times (42)
Rnd 7 (dc6, dc2 into next st) 6 times (48)
Rnd 8 (dc7, dc2 into next st) 6 times (54)
Rnds 9–13 dc (5 rnds)
Rnd 14 (dc7, dc2tog) 6 times (48)
Rnd 15 (dc6, dc2tog) 6 times (42)
Rnd 16 (dc5, dc2tog) 6 times (36)
Rnd 17 (dc4, dc2tog) 6 times (30)
Rnd 18 (dc3, dc2tog) 6 times (24)
Rnd 19 (dc2, dc2tog) 6 times (18)
Rnd 20 (dc2tog) 9 times (9)
Change to Lime
Rnds 21–22 dc (2 rnds)
Rnd 23 (dc2 into next st) 9 times (18)
Rnd 24 (dc2, dc2 into next st) 6 times (24)
Rnds 25–30 dc (6 rnds)

Rnd 31 (dc3, dc2 into next st) 6 times (30)
Rnds 32–34 dc (3 rnds)
Rnd 35 (dc4, dc2 into next st) 6 times (36)
Rnd 36 dc12, (dc1, dc2 into next st) 6 times, dc12 (42)
Rnd 37 (dc6, dc2 into next st) 6 times (48)
Rnds 38–42 dc (5 rnds)
Rnd 43 (dc6, dc2tog) 6 times (42)
Rnd 44 (dc5, dc2tog) 6 times (36)
Rnd 45 dc
Rnd 46 (dc4, dc2tog) 6 times (30)
Rnd 47 (dc3, dc2tog) 6 times (24)
Rnd 48 (dc2, dc2tog) 6 times (18)
Rnd 49 (dc2tog) 9 times (9)

ARMS (make two)
Working in Lime
Ch12 and sl st to join into a circle
Rnds 1–20 dc (20 rnds)
Rnd 21 (dc5, dc2 into next st) twice (14)
Rnd 22 (dc6, dc2 into next st) twice (16)
Rnd 23 (dc7, dc2 into next st) twice (18)
Rnds 24–29 dc (6 rnds)
Continues overleaf

MADE IN Lime and Violet
YARN QUANTITIES 50g foliage, 75g flower
TIME TO GROW Speedy grower
COLOUR VARIANTS Blue, Amethyst, Violet
REQUIRES htr, tr

Rnd 30 (dc7, dc2tog) twice (16)
Rnd 31 (dc6, dc2tog) twice (14)
Rnd 32 (dc5, dc2tog) twice (12)
Rnd 33 (dc4, dc2tog) twice (10)
Rnd 34 (dc3, dc2tog) twice (8)
Rnd 35 (dc2, dc2tog) twice (6)
Rnd 36 (dc1, dc2tog) twice (4)
Stuff end lightly and sew flat across top to close.

LEGS (make two)
Working in Lime
Ch12 and sl st to join into a circle
Rnds 1–35 dc (35 rnds)
Rnd 36 (dc2tog) 6 times (6)
Stuff foot and sew flat across top to close.

HOOD
Working in Violet
Begin by dc6 into ring
Rnd 1 (dc2 into next st) 6 times (12)
Rnd 2 (dc1, dc2 into next st) 6 times (18)

Rnd 3 (dc2, dc2 into next st) 6 times (24)
Rnd 4 (dc3, dc2 into next st) 6 times (30)
Rnd 5 (dc4, dc2 into next st) 6 times (36)
Rnd 6 (dc5, dc2 into next st) 6 times (42)
Rnd 7 (dc6, dc2 into next st) 6 times (48)
Rnd 8 dc
Ch8, miss 8 sts and then dc40 to end of rnd
Rnd 9 dc8 on chain, dc40 (48)
Rnds 10–16 dc (7 rnds)
Rnd 17 (dc6, dc2tog) 6 times (42)
Rnds 18–25 dc (8 rnds)
Rnd 26 (dc6, dc2 into next st) 6 times (48)
Rnd 27 [dc2 into next st, (htr2 into next st) twice, (tr2 into next st) twice, (htr2 into next st) twice, dc2 into next st] 6 times (96)
Rnd 28 (dc2, htr5, tr2, htr5, dc2) 6 times

Add flower hood before stuffing (see page 155).

Finish by sewing eyes into place with Black and Cream yarn.

Peony

An absolute showstopper in the garden in late Spring, the beautiful peony is reminiscent of hand-rolled balls of yarn before you even crochet a stitch! The peony symbolises bashfulness and compassion, and pink peonies are some of the most commonly gifted flowers. They represent the beauty of marriage and are often used in floral bouquets at weddings. Peonies are native to China and there are associated with royalty, symbolising honour, riches and prosperity. Much like other yellow flowers, yellow peonies stand for new beginnings, and thus are the perfect flower to make to warm a friend's new home.

HEAD/BODY
Working in Peony
Begin by dc6 into ring
Rnd 1 (dc2 into next st) 6 times (12 sts)
Rnd 2 (dc1, dc2 into next st) 6 times (18)
Rnd 3 (dc2, dc2 into next st) 6 times (24)
Rnd 4 (dc3, dc2 into next st) 6 times (30)
Rnd 5 (dc4, dc2 into next st) 6 times (36)
Rnd 6 (dc5, dc2 into next st) 6 times (42)
Rnd 7 (dc6, dc2 into next st) 6 times (48)
Rnd 8 (dc7, dc2 into next st) 6 times (54)
Rnds 9–16 dc (8 rnds)
Rnd 17 (dc7, dc2tog) 6 times (48)
Rnd 18 (dc6, dc2tog) 6 times (42)
Rnd 19 (dc5, dc2tog) 6 times (36)
Rnd 20 (dc4, dc2tog) 6 times (30)
Rnd 21 (dc3, dc2tog) 6 times (24)
Rnd 22 (dc2, dc2tog) 6 times (18)
Rnd 23 (dc2tog) 9 times (9)
Change to Lime
Rnds 24–25 dc (2 rnds)
Rnd 26 (dc2 into next st) 9 times (18)
Rnd 27 (dc2, dc2 into next st) 6 times (24)

Rnds 28–33 dc (6 rnds)
Rnd 34 (dc3, dc2 into next st) 6 times (30)
Rnds 35–37 dc (3 rnds)
Rnd 38 (dc4, dc2 into next st) 6 times (36)
Rnd 39 dc12, (dc1, dc2 into next st) 6 times, dc12 (42)
Rnd 40 (dc6, dc2 into next st) 6 times (48)
Rnds 41–45 dc (5 rnds)
Rnd 46 (dc6, dc2tog) 6 times (42)
Rnd 47 (dc5, dc2tog) 6 times (36)
Rnd 48 dc
Rnd 49 (dc4, dc2tog) 6 times (30)
Rnd 50 (dc3, dc2tog) 6 times (24)
Rnd 51 (dc2, dc2tog) 6 times (18)
Rnd 52 (dc2tog) 9 times (9)

ARMS (make two)
Working in Lime
Ch12 and sl st to join into a circle
Rnds 1–15 dc (15 rnds)
Rnd 16 (dc1, dc2 into next st) 6 times (18)
Rnd 17 (dc2, dc2 into next st) 6 times (24)
Continues overleaf

MADE IN Lime and Peony (overleaf with Primrose flower)
YARN QUANTITIES 50g foliage, 75g flower
TIME TO GROW Moderate
COLOUR VARIANTS Pink, Magenta, Primrose, Yellow, Coral, Orange, Cream
REQUIRES htr, tr, dtr, splitting the round (see illustration 2, page 33)

Count 8 sts back, split these sts into an 8-st rnd and work as follows:
Rnd 1 dc
Rnd 2 (dc1, dc2 into next st) 4 times (12)

Dc3, count 6 sts back, split these 6 sts and dc3. Work this 6-st rnd as follows:
Rnds 1–2 dc (2 rnds)
Rnd 3 (dc1, dc2tog) twice (4)
Break yarn.
Rejoin on remaining 6 sts and work as follows:
Rnd 1 dc
Rnd 2 (dc1, dc2tog) twice (4)
Break yarn.

Miss 4 sts along main stem, rejoin and dc8, split these sts into an 8-st round and work as follows:
Rnd 1 (dc1, dc2 into next st) 4 times (12)

Dc3, count 6 sts back, split these 6 sts and dc3. Work this 6-st rnd as follows:
Rnds 1–2 dc (2 rnds)
Rnd 3 (dc1, dc2tog) twice (4)
Break yarn.
Rejoin on remaining 6 sts and work as follows:
Rnd 1 dc
Rnd 2 (dc1, dc2tog) twice (4)
Break yarn.

Rejoin and work central 8-st round as follows (4 sts from each side):
Rnds 1–6 dc (6 rnds)
Rnd 7 (dc1, dc2 into next st) 4 times (12)
Rnd 8 (dc1, dc2 into next st) 6 times (18)

Dc3, count 6 sts back, split these sts into a 6-st round and work as follows:
Rnd 1 dc
Rnd 2 (dc1, dc2tog) twice (4)
Break yarn.
Miss 3 central sts, dc6, split these sts into a 6-st round and work as follows:
Rnd 1 dc
Rnd 2 (dc1, dc2tog) twice (4)
Break yarn.
Rejoin and work central 6-st round as follows (3 sts from each side):
Rnds 1–3 dc (3 rnds)

Rnd 4 (dc1, dc2tog) twice (4)
Break yarn.
Stuff end lightly and sew flat across top to close.

LEGS (make two)
Working in Lime
Ch12 and sl st to join into a circle
Rnds 1–35 dc (35 rnds)
Rnd 36 (dc2tog) 6 times (6)
Stuff foot and sew flat across top to close.

EDGE PETALS (make four)
Working in Peony
The edge petals are made separately and then sewn around the head at the end.
Rnd 1 ch4, tr9 into first ch, sl st into top of ch to join (10)
Rnd 2 ch2, (tr2 into next st) 9 times, tr1, sl st into top of ch to join (20)
Rnd 3 ch2, (tr1, tr2 into next st) 6 times, (dtr4 into next st) 8 times, sl st into top of first st to join (50)
Sew into position around bottom of head.

TIP: The chain at the start of each round counts as a stitch (see page 23 for chart).

INNER PETALS
The following petals are worked directly into the head, working along nine head stitches as instructed. Some peonies have multiple rows of petals emerging from the crown; others have single circles of outer petals with feathery centres. Once you have sewn your edge petals into an upright position above the bottom of the head, work as many of the below as desired from the outside, moving towards the centre.

Sl st into position, ch2 (tr1, dtr1) into same st as ch, (dtr4 into next st) 5 times (dtr1, tr2) into next st, sl st to join.

Complete the centre of the flower with ch7 SLIP ST CHAINS (see page 154) as desired.

Finish by sewing eyes into place with Black and Cream yarn.

Chrysanthemum

These flowers have been cultivated to cover the whole colour spectrum, with the exception of a bold blue, and this is a pattern you can make quickly, over and over again. In Asia, the chrysanthemum signifies life and rebirth, making these flowers great gifts for all birthdays and baby showers. In Europe, by contrast, the chrysanthemum more often signifies an expression of sympathy, and is associated with death, so has become a popular graveside flower. In some cultures, it is even thought that chrysanthemums have magical powers, so they are planted in gardens, kept in vases in homes and even burned as incense, in the hope of warding off evil spirits and attracting good fortune.

HEAD/BODY
Working in Pink
Begin by dc6 into ring
Rnd 1 (dc2 into next st) 6 times (12 sts)
Rnd 2 (dc1, dc2 into next st) 6 times (18)
Rnd 3 (dc2, dc2 into next st) 6 times (24)
Rnd 4 (dc3, dc2 into next st) 6 times (30)
Rnd 5 (dc4, dc2 into next st) 6 times (36)
Rnd 6 (dc5, dc2 into next st) 6 times (42)
Rnd 7 (dc6, dc2 into next st) 6 times (48)
Rnd 8 (dc7, dc2 into next st) 6 times (54)
Rnds 9–13 dc (5 rnds)
Rnd 14 (dc7, dc2tog) 6 times (48)
Rnd 15 (dc6, dc2tog) 6 times (42)
Rnd 16 (dc5, dc2tog) 6 times (36)
Rnd 17 (dc4, dc2tog) 6 times (30)
Rnd 18 (dc3, dc2tog) 6 times (24)
Rnd 19 (dc2, dc2tog) 6 times (18)
Rnd 20 (dc2tog) 9 times (9)
Change to Lime
Rnds 21–22 dc (2 rnds)
Rnd 23 (dc2 into next st) 9 times (18)

Rnd 24 (dc2, dc2 into next st) 6 times (24)
Rnds 25–30 dc (6 rnds)
Rnd 31 (dc3, dc2 into next st) 6 times (30)
Rnds 32–34 dc (3 rnds)
Rnd 35 (dc4, dc2 into next st) 6 times (36)
Rnd 36 dc12, (dc1, dc2 into next st) 6 times, dc12 (42)
Rnd 37 (dc6, dc2 into next st) 6 times (48)
Rnds 38–42 dc (5 rnds)
Rnd 43 (dc6, dc2tog) 6 times (42)
Rnd 44 (dc5, dc2tog) 6 times (36)
Rnd 45 dc
Rnd 46 (dc4, dc2tog) 6 times (30)
Rnd 47 (dc3, dc2tog) 6 times (24)
Rnd 48 (dc2, dc2tog) 6 times (18)
Rnd 49 (dc2tog) 9 times (9)

ARMS (make two)
Working in Lime
Ch12 and sl st to join into a circle
Rnds 1–20 dc (20 rnds)
Continues overleaf

MADE IN Lime and Pink (overleaf with Primrose flower)
YARN QUANTITIES 50g foliage, 75g flower
TIME TO GROW Moderate
COLOUR VARIANTS Peony, Coral, Primrose, Magenta, Ruby
REQUIRES Slip stitch chain

Rnd 21 (dc5, dc2 into next st) twice (14)
Rnd 22 (dc6, dc2 into next st) twice (16)
Rnd 23 (dc7, dc2 into next st) twice (18)
Rnds 24–29 dc (6 rnds)
Rnd 30 (dc7, dc2tog) twice (16)
Rnd 31 (dc6, dc2tog) twice (14)
Rnd 32 (dc5, dc2tog) twice (12)
Rnd 33 (dc4, dc2tog) twice (10)
Rnd 34 (dc3, dc2tog) twice (8)
Rnd 35 (dc2, dc2tog) twice (6)
Rnd 36 (dc1, dc2tog) twice (4)
Stuff end lightly and sew flat across top to close.

LEGS (make two)
Working in Lime
Ch12 and sl st to join into a circle

Rnds 1–35 dc (35 rnds)
Rnd 36 (dc2tog) 6 times (6)
Stuff foot and sew flat across top to close.

PETALS
Working in Pink
Working from front to back and leaving face and back of head plain, work three rnds of ch10 SLIP STITCH CHAINS (see page 154) around head.
Next, work one rnd of ch12 SLIP STITCH CHAINS (there will be approximately 24 petals per round).

Finish by sewing eyes into place with Black and Cream yarn.

Alstroemeria

The alstroemeria or 'Peruvian Lily' is symbolic of wealth, prosperity and fortune, but is also a flower with the message of friendship. Associated with the achievement of aspirations, it is the perfect good luck gift or token of companionship to accompany someone on a challenge they face without you at their side. An alstroemeria represents mutual support and the ability to help each other through the difficulties life throws at us, making it the perfect flower to crochet for your best friend when they are in need of a pick-me-up.

HEAD/BODY
Working in Orange
Begin by dc6 into ring
Rnd 1 (dc2 into next st) 6 times (12 sts)
Rnd 2 (dc1, dc2 into next st) 6 times (18)
Rnd 3 (dc2, dc2 into next st) 6 times (24)
Rnd 4 (dc3, dc2 into next st) 6 times (30)
Rnd 5 (dc4, dc2 into next st) 6 times (36)
Rnd 6 (dc5, dc2 into next st) 6 times (42)
Rnd 7 (dc6, dc2 into next st) 6 times (48)
Rnd 8 (dc7, dc2 into next st) 6 times (54)
Rnds 9–13 dc (5 rnds)
Rnd 14 (dc7, dc2tog) 6 times (48)
Rnd 15 (dc6, dc2tog) 6 times (42)
Rnd 16 (dc5, dc2tog) 6 times (36)
Rnd 17 (dc4, dc2tog) 6 times (30)
Rnd 18 (dc3, dc2tog) 6 times (24)
Rnd 19 (dc2, dc2tog) 6 times (18)
Rnd 20 (dc2tog) 9 times (9)
Change to Green
Rnds 21–22 dc (2 rnds)
Rnd 23 (dc2 into next st) 9 times (18)
Rnd 24 (dc2, dc2 into next st) 6 times (24)
Rnds 25–30 dc (6 rnds)

Rnd 31 (dc3, dc2 into next st) 6 times (30)
Rnds 32–34 dc (3 rnds)
Rnd 35 (dc4, dc2 into next st) 6 times (36)
Rnd 36 dc12, (dc1, dc2 into next st) 6 times, dc12 (42)
Rnd 37 (dc6, dc2 into next st) 6 times (48)
Rnds 38–42 dc (5 rnds)
Rnd 43 (dc6, dc2tog) 6 times (42)
Rnd 44 (dc5, dc2tog) 6 times (36)
Rnd 45 dc
Rnd 46 (dc4, dc2tog) 6 times (30)
Rnd 47 (dc3, dc2tog) 6 times (24)
Rnd 48 (dc2, dc2tog) 6 times (18)
Rnd 49 (dc2tog) 9 times (9)

ARMS (make two)
Working in Green
Ch12 and sl st to join into a circle
Rnds 1–20 dc (20 rnds)
Rnd 21 (dc5, dc2 into next st) twice (14)
Rnd 22 (dc6, dc2 into next st) twice (16)
Rnd 23 (dc7, dc2 into next st) twice (18)
Rnds 24–29 dc (6 rnds)
Continues overleaf

MADE IN Green, Orange, Yellow and Cocoa (overleaf with Pink, Peony and Magenta flower)
YARN QUANTITIES 50g foliage, 50g flower, 25g flower contrast, 25g marking contrast
TIME TO GROW Moderate
COLOUR VARIANTS Pink, Magenta, Ruby, Cream, Peony
REQUIRES Splitting the round (see illustration 2, page 33), slip stitch chain, embroidery

Rnd 30 (dc7, dc2tog) twice (16)
Rnd 31 (dc6, dc2tog) twice (14)
Rnd 32 (dc5, dc2tog) twice (12)
Rnd 33 (dc4, dc2tog) twice (10)
Rnd 34 (dc3, dc2tog) twice (8)
Rnd 35 (dc2, dc2tog) twice (6)
Rnd 36 (dc1, dc2tog) twice (4)
Stuff end lightly and sew flat across top to close.

LEGS (make two)
Working in Green
Ch12 and sl st to join into a circle
Rnds 1–35 dc (35 rnds)
Rnd 36 (dc2tog) 6 times (6)
Stuff foot and sew flat across top to close.

BASE PETALS (make three)
Working in Orange
Ch20 and sl st to join into a circle
Rnd 1 (dc4, dc2 into next st) 4 times (24)
Rnd 2 (dc3, dc2 into next st) 6 times (30)
Rnd 3 (dc4, dc2 into next st) 6 times (36)
Rnds 4–13 dc (10 rnds)
Split into two rnds of 18 sts and work each as
    follows:
Rnds 1–2 dc (2 rnds)
Rnd 3 (dc4, dc2tog) 3 times (15)
Rnd 4 (dc1, dc2tog) 5 times (10)
Do not stuff.

PATTERNED PETALS (make three)
Working in Yellow
Ch20 and sl st to join into a circle
Rnd 1 (dc4, dc2 into next st) 4 times (24)
Rnds 2–8 dc (7 rnds)
Rnd 9 (dc3, dc2 into next st) 6 times (30)
Rnds 10–12 dc (3 rnds)
Rnd 13 (dc8, dc2tog) 3 times (27)

Rnd 14 (dc7, dc2tog) 3 times (24)
Rnd 15 (dc6, dc2tog) 3 times (21)
Rnd 16 (dc5, dc2tog) 3 times (18)
Rnd 17 (dc1, dc2tog) 6 times (12)
Rnd 18 (dc2tog) 6 times (6)
Do not stuff.

Make a ring of petals with your BASE PETALS
    by dc along the bottom of each petal with
    ch4 between each petal. Make a second
    ring of petals with the PATTERNED PETALS
    by dc across the bottom of two immediately
    together and then ch6 either side of the
    third petal.
Sew into position on head (see pages 152–153).

Working in Cocoa
Oversew short lines onto the PATTERNED
    PETALS, making sure to keep the stitches
    visible on the front only (see page 156).

STAMEN FILAMENT
Working in Cocoa
Sl st into position on top of head
Work two ch12 SLIP STITCH CHAINS (see
    page 154) and one ch18 SLIP STITCH
    CHAIN.

STAMEN ANTHER (make three)
Working in Yellow
Sl st into position on end of each STAMEN
    FILAMENT
Ch2, tr4 into end
Break yarn, gather edge sts and sew in ends.

Finish by sewing eyes into place with Black and
    Cream yarn.

Rose

Although best known for its association with romantic love, the colour you choose to make your rose in can drastically change the message. Since ancient times, roses have been grown for their fragrance, beauty and healing properties. With their perfect combination of thorned stems and beautiful, delicate, fragrant flowers, roses are often prized as emblems of achievement, completion and perfection in gardening and in life. Red roses symbolise romance, love, beauty and courage and, interestingly, a thornless red rose means love at first sight. Yellow roses convey friendship, joy and new beginnings, whereas the more unusual orange rose symbolises fascination and sensuality. Pink roses indicate appreciation and gratitude, whereas the classic bridal choice of a white rose stands for innocence and purity, but can also mean silence and secrecy. This is a pattern that works for every occasion.

HEAD/BODY
Working in Ruby
Begin by dc6 into ring
Rnd 1 (dc2 into next st) 6 times (12 sts)
Rnd 2 (dc1, dc2 into next st) 6 times (18)
Rnd 3 (dc2, dc2 into next st) 6 times (24)
Rnd 4 (dc3, dc2 into next st) 6 times (30)
Rnd 5 (dc4, dc2 into next st) 6 times (36)
Rnd 6 (dc5, dc2 into next st) 6 times (42)
Rnd 7 (dc6, dc2 into next st) 6 times (48)
Rnd 8 (dc7, dc2 into next st) 6 times (54)
Rnds 9–13 dc (5 rnds)
Rnd 14 (dc7, dc2tog) 6 times (48)
Rnd 15 (dc6, dc2tog) 6 times (42)
Rnd 16 (dc5, dc2tog) 6 times (36)
Rnd 17 (dc4, dc2tog) 6 times (30)
Rnd 18 (dc3, dc2tog) 6 times (24)
Rnd 19 (dc2, dc2tog) 6 times (18)

Rnd 20 (dc2tog) 9 times (9)
Change to Green
Rnds 21–22 dc (2 rnds)
Rnd 23 (dc2 into next st) 9 times (18)
Rnd 24 (dc2, dc2 into next st) 6 times (24)
Rnds 25–30 dc (6 rnds)
Rnd 31 (dc3, dc2 into next st) 6 times (30)
Rnds 32–34 dc (3 rnds)
Rnd 35 (dc4, dc2 into next st) 6 times (36)
Rnd 36 dc12, (dc1, dc2 into next st) 6 times, dc12 (42)
Rnd 37 (dc6, dc2 into next st) 6 times (48)
Rnds 38–42 dc (5 rnds)
Rnd 43 (dc6, dc2tog) 6 times (42)
Rnd 44 (dc5, dc2tog) 6 times (36)
Rnd 45 dc
Rnd 46 (dc4, dc2tog) 6 times (30)
Continues overleaf

MADE IN Green and Ruby (overleaf with Pink flower)
YARN QUANTITIES 50g foliage, 75g flower
TIME TO GROW Moderate
COLOUR VARIANTS Pink, Magenta, Cream, Peony, Yellow, Primrose, Coral, Violet
REQUIRES htr, tr

Rnd 47 (dc3, dc2tog) 6 times (24)
Rnd 48 (dc2, dc2tog) 6 times (18)
Rnd 49 (dc2tog) 9 times (9)

ARMS (make two)
Working in Green
Begin by dc6 into ring
Rnd 1 (dc2, dc2 into next st) twice (8)
Rnds 2–33 dc (32 rnds)
Stuff end lightly and sew flat across top to close.

LEGS (make two)
Working in Green
Ch12 and sl st to join into a circle
Rnds 1–35 dc (35 rnds)
Rnd 36 (dc2tog) 6 times (6)
Stuff foot and sew flat across top to close.

LEAVES (make six)
Working in Green
Begin by dc6 into ring
Rnd 1 (dc2 into next st) 6 times (12)
Rnd 2 (dc1, dc2 into next st) 6 times (18)
Rnds 3–7 dc (5 rnds)
Rnd 8 (dc4, dc2tog) 3 times (15)
Rnd 9 dc
Rnd 10 (dc3, dc2tog) 3 times (12)
Rnd 11 dc
Rnd 12 (dc1, dc2tog) 4 times (8)
Rnd 13 dc
Rnd 14 (dc2, dc2tog) twice (6)
Do not stuff. Sew into position on arms.

OUTER PETALS (make four)
Working in Ruby
Begin by dc6 into ring
Rnd 1 (dc2 into next st) 6 times (12)
Rnd 2 (dc1, dc2 into next st) 6 times (18)
Rnd 3 (dc2, dc2 into next st) 6 times (24)
Rnd 4 (dc3, dc2 into next st) 6 times (30)
Rnd 5 (dc4, dc2 into next st) 6 times (36)
Rnd 6 (dc5, dc2 into next st) 6 times (42)
Rnd 7 dc3, htr3, tr2 into next st, tr4, tr2 into
    next st, htr3, dc27 (44)

Rnd 8 dc3, htr3, tr2 into next st, tr4, tr2 into
    next st, htr3, dc3 (incomplete rnd)

CENTRE
Working in Ruby
Ch10, turn and work back down chain
    as follows:
dc1, htr1, tr5, htr1, dc1

CENTRE CIRCLE
Working in Ruby
Ch27 and sl st to join into a circle
Rnd 1 (dc1, htr1, tr5, htr1, sl st1) 3 times

INNER PETALS (make four)
Working in Ruby
Ch14, turn and work back down chain
    as follows:
dc2, htr2, tr5, htr2, dc2

SEWING UP PETALS
1. Sew the OUTER PETALS around the edge
   of the head, sewing two opposite petals first
   and the second two overlapping the first
   ones. The treble sts are the top of the petal.
2. Sew the CENTRE onto the centre of the top
   of the head.
3. Sew the CENTRE CIRCLE on the top of the
   head, around the CENTRE.
4. Sew the four INNER PETALS around the
   head, between the OUTER PETALS and
   CENTRE CIRCLE.

SEPAL
Working in Green
Once all sewn up, sl st into position on neck at
    colour change rnd.
*Ch13, turn and work back down chain as
    follows:
sl st3, dc3, htr3, tr3, sl st into neck
Repeat from * three more times around neck.

Finish by sewing eyes into place with Black and
    Cream yarn.

Petunia

Although typically given as a potted plant, petunias still have lots of different meanings. Anger and resentment are common themes associated with this flower, so when it is given to someone with whom you have recently had an argument, the petunia becomes the peacemaker. A petunia also signifies the desire never to lose hope. As in so many cases, the colour can alter the meaning of the message. Purple petunias symbolise fantasy and mystery with magical connotations, whereas a blue petunia conveys peacefulness and intimacy and can be a symbol of a deep trust shared between people.

HEAD/BODY
Working in Cream
Begin by dc6 into ring
Rnd 1 (dc2 into next st) 6 times (12 sts)
Rnd 2 (dc1, dc2 into next st) 6 times (18)
Rnd 3 (dc2, dc2 into next st) 6 times (24)
Rnd 4 (dc3, dc2 into next st) 6 times (30)
Rnd 5 (dc4, dc2 into next st) 6 times (36)
Rnd 6 (dc5, dc2 into next st) 6 times (42)
Rnd 7 (dc6, dc2 into next st) 6 times (48)
Rnd 8 (dc7, dc2 into next st) 6 times (54)
Rnds 9–13 dc (5 rnds)
Rnd 14 (dc7, dc2tog) 6 times (48)
Rnd 15 (dc6, dc2tog) 6 times (42)
Rnd 16 (dc5, dc2tog) 6 times (36)
Rnd 17 (dc4, dc2tog) 6 times (30)
Rnd 18 (dc3, dc2tog) 6 times (24)
Rnd 19 (dc2, dc2tog) 6 times (18)
Rnd 20 (dc2tog) 9 times (9)
Change to Green
Rnds 21–22 dc (2 rnds)
Rnd 23 (dc2 into next st) 9 times (18)
Rnd 24 (dc2, dc2 into next st) 6 times (24)

Rnds 25–30 dc (6 rnds)
Rnd 31 (dc3, dc2 into next st) 6 times (30)
Rnds 32–34 dc (3 rnds)
Rnd 35 (dc4, dc2 into next st) 6 times (36)
Rnd 36 dc12, (dc1, dc2 into next st) 6 times, dc12 (42)
Rnd 37 (dc6, dc2 into next st) 6 times (48)
Rnds 38–42 dc (5 rnds)
Rnd 43 (dc6, dc2tog) 6 times (42)
Rnd 44 (dc5, dc2tog) 6 times (36)
Rnd 45 dc
Rnd 46 (dc4, dc2tog) 6 times (30)
Rnd 47 (dc3, dc2tog) 6 times (24)
Rnd 48 (dc2, dc2tog) 6 times (18)
Rnd 49 (dc2tog) 9 times (9)

ARMS (make two)
Working in Green
Ch12 and sl st to join into a circle
Rnds 1–20 dc (20 rnds)
Rnd 21 (dc5, dc2 into next st) twice (14)
Rnd 22 (dc6, dc2 into next st) twice (16)
Continues overleaf

MADE IN Green, Magenta and Cream (overleaf with Amethyst flower)
YARN QUANTITIES 50g foliage, 50g flower, 25g flower contrast
TIME TO GROW Speedy grower
COLOUR VARIANTS Pink, Magenta, Amethyst, Ruby
REQUIRES htr, tr

Rnd 23 (dc7, dc2 into next st) twice (18)
Rnds 24–29 dc (6 rnds)
Rnd 30 (dc7, dc2tog) twice (16)
Rnd 31 (dc6, dc2tog) twice (14)
Rnd 32 (dc5, dc2tog) twice (12)
Rnd 33 (dc4, dc2tog) twice (10)
Rnd 34 (dc3, dc2tog) twice (8)
Rnd 35 (dc2, dc2tog) twice (6)
Rnd 36 (dc1, dc2tog) twice (4)
Stuff end lightly and sew flat across top to close.

LEGS (make two)
Working in Green
Ch12 and sl st to join into a circle
Rnds 1–35 dc (35 rnds)
Rnd 36 (dc2tog) 6 times (6)
Stuff foot and sew flat across top to close.

PETAL HOOD
Working in Magenta
Begin by dc6 into ring
Rnd 1 (dc2 into next st) 6 times (12)
Rnd 2 (dc1, dc2 into next st) 6 times (18)
Rnd 3 (dc2, dc2 into next st) 6 times (24)
Rnd 4 (dc3, dc2 into next st) 6 times (30)
Rnd 5 (dc4, dc2 into next st) 6 times (36)
Rnd 6 (dc5, dc2 into next st) 6 times (42)
Rnd 7 (dc6, dc2 into next st) 6 times (48)
Rnds 8–10 dc (3 rnds)
Rnd 11 dc40, ch8, miss 8 sts
Rnd 12 dc40, dc8 in chain (48)
Rnds 13–17 dc (5 rnds)

Rnd 18 (dc6, dc2tog) 6 times (42)
Rnd 19 dc
Rnd 20 (dc6, dc2 into next st) 6 times (48)
Rnd 21 (dc7, dc2 into next st) 6 times (54)
Rnd 22 (dc8, dc2 into next st) 6 times (60)
Rnd 23 (dc2 into next st, dc11) 5 times (65)
Rnd 24 (dc2 into next st, dc12) 5 times (70)
Rnd 25 tr1, htr3, dc6, htr3, tr2, (htr3, dc6, htr3, tr2) 3 times, htr3, dc6, htr3, tr1
Rnd 26 (dc13, dc2 into next st) 5 times (75)

Add hood before stuffing (see page 155).

STAR (make five; see chart)
Working in Cream
Ch13
Rnd 1 dc1, htr2, tr6, htr2, dc1, ch1 along one side of chain, dc1, htr2, tr6, htr2, dc1 along other side of chain
Sew into position around hood.

Finish by sewing eyes into place with Black and Cream yarn.

Fuchsia

The fuchsia – also known as 'lady's eardrops' – signifies confiding love, and so can be used as a way of expressing your trust in someone. There are more than 100 species of fuchsia, in a myriad of pinks, purples and reds. It was named after 16th-century botanist Leonhart Fuchs. Over time, the fuchsia came to be seen as an enchanted plant, and it was hung outside doorways to help protect those who lived inside.

HEAD/BODY

Working in Magenta

Begin by dc6 into ring

Rnd 1 (dc2 into next st) 6 times (12 sts)
Rnd 2 (dc1, dc2 into next st) 6 times (18)
Rnd 3 (dc2, dc2 into next st) 6 times (24)
Rnd 4 (dc3, dc2 into next st) 6 times (30)
Rnd 5 (dc4, dc2 into next st) 6 times (36)
Rnd 6 (dc5, dc2 into next st) 6 times (42)
Rnd 7 (dc6, dc2 into next st) 6 times (48)
Rnd 8 (dc7, dc2 into next st) 6 times (54)
Rnds 9–13 dc (5 rnds)
Rnd 14 (dc7, dc2tog) 6 times (48)
Rnd 15 (dc6, dc2tog) 6 times (42)
Rnd 16 (dc5, dc2tog) 6 times (36)
Rnd 17 (dc4, dc2tog) 6 times (30)
Rnd 18 (dc3, dc2tog) 6 times (24)
Rnd 19 (dc2, dc2tog) 6 times (18)
Rnd 20 (dc2tog) 9 times (9)
Change to Lime
Rnds 21–22 dc (2 rnds)
Rnd 23 (dc2 into next st) 9 times (18)
Rnd 24 (dc2, dc2 into next st) 6 times (24)
Rnds 25–30 dc (6 rnds)
Rnd 31 (dc3, dc2 into next st) 6 times (30)

Rnds 32–34 dc (3 rnds)
Rnd 35 (dc4, dc2 into next st) 6 times (36)
Rnd 36 dc12, (dc1, dc2 into next st) 6 times, dc12 (42)
Rnd 37 (dc6, dc2 into next st) 6 times (48)
Rnds 38–42 dc (5 rnds)
Rnd 43 (dc6, dc2tog) 6 times (42)
Rnd 44 (dc5, dc2tog) 6 times (36)
Rnd 45 dc
Rnd 46 (dc4, dc2tog) 6 times (30)
Rnd 47 (dc3, dc2tog) 6 times (24)
Rnd 48 (dc2, dc2tog) 6 times (18)
Rnd 49 (dc2tog) 9 times (9)

ARMS (make two)

Working in Lime

Ch12 and sl st to join into a circle

Rnds 1–20 dc (20 rnds)
Rnd 21 (dc5, dc2 into next st) twice (14)
Rnd 22 (dc6, dc2 into next st) twice (16)
Rnd 23 (dc7, dc2 into next st) twice (18)
Rnds 24–29 dc (6 rnds)
Rnd 30 (dc7, dc2tog) twice (16)
Rnd 31 (dc6, dc2tog) twice (14)
Continues overleaf

MADE IN Lime, Pink and Magenta (overleaf with Magenta and Amethyst flower)
YARN QUANTITIES 50g foliage, 50g flower, 25g flower contrast
TIME TO GROW Moderate
COLOUR VARIANTS Pink, Magenta, Amethyst, Cream, Peony
REQUIRES Slip stitch chain

Rnd 32 (dc5, dc2tog) twice (12)
Rnd 33 (dc4, dc2tog) twice (10)
Rnd 34 (dc3, dc2tog) twice (8)
Rnd 35 (dc2, dc2tog) twice (6)
Rnd 36 (dc1, dc2tog) twice (4)
Stuff end lightly and sew flat across top to close.

LEGS (make two)
Working in Lime
Ch12 and sl st to join into a circle
Rnds 1–35 dc (35 rnds)
Rnd 36 (dc2tog) 6 times (6)
Stuff foot and sew flat across top to close.

PETALS (make four)
Working in Pink
Ch24 and sl st to join into a circle
Rnds 1–5 dc (5 rnds)
Rnd 6 (dc3, dc2 into next st) 6 times (30)
Rnds 7–15 dc (9 rnds)
Rnd 16 (dc2tog, dc8) 3 times (27)
Rnd 17 (dc2tog, dc7) 3 times (24)
Rnd 18 (dc2tog, dc6) 3 times (21)
Rnd 19 (dc2tog, dc5) 3 times (18)
Rnd 20 (dc2tog, dc4) 3 times (15)
Rnd 21 (dc2tog, dc3) 3 times (12)
Rnd 22 (dc2tog, dc2) 3 times (9)

Make two rings of petals by dc along
    bottom of each petal with a ch9 in
    between each petal.
Sew into position on head (see pages 152–153).

STAMEN FILAMENT
Working in Pink
Sl st into position on top of head
Work three ch24 SLIP STITCH CHAINS (see
    page 154).

STAMEN ANTHER (make three)
Working in Magenta
Begin by dc6 into ring
Rnds 1–2 dc (2 rnds)
Gather sts and sew into position on end of
    STAMEN FILAMENT.

PISTIL STYLE
Working in Pink
Sl st into position on top of head
Work one ch36 SLIP STITCH CHAIN.

PISTIL STIGMA (make one)
Working in Magenta
Begin by dc6 into ring
Rnd 1 (dc1, dc2 into next st) 3 times (9)
Rnds 2–3 dc (2 rnds)
Rnd 4 (dc1, dc2tog) 3 times (6)
Gather sts and sew into position on end of
    PISTIL STYLE.

Finish by sewing eyes into place with Black and
    Cream yarn.

Hydrangea

The hydrangea is an interesting plant because the flower colour largely depends on the pH of the soil in which it is grown. Acidic soil contains more aluminium so the flowers turn blue, whereas alkaline soil heavy in lime produces pink flowers. The hydrangea can represent heartlessness, and Victorian men sent hydrangeas to women who had turned them down. However, it can also represent sincerity, or gratitude for being understood or listened to, so it is a plant with many mixed meanings.

HEAD/BODY
Working in Pink
Begin by dc6 into ring
Rnd 1 (dc2 into next st) 6 times (12 sts)
Rnd 2 (dc1, dc2 into next st) 6 times (18)
Rnd 3 (dc2, dc2 into next st) 6 times (24)
Rnd 4 (dc3, dc2 into next st) 6 times (30)
Rnd 5 (dc4, dc2 into next st) 6 times (36)
Rnd 6 (dc5, dc2 into next st) 6 times (42)
Rnd 7 (dc6, dc2 into next st) 6 times (48)
Rnd 8 (dc7, dc2 into next st) 6 times (54)
Rnds 9–13 dc (5 rnds)
Rnd 14 (dc7, dc2tog) 6 times (48)
Rnd 15 (dc6, dc2tog) 6 times (42)
Rnd 16 (dc5, dc2tog) 6 times (36)
Rnd 17 (dc4, dc2tog) 6 times (30)
Rnd 18 (dc3, dc2tog) 6 times (24)
Rnd 19 (dc2, dc2tog) 6 times (18)
Rnd 20 (dc2tog) 9 times (9)
Change to Green
Rnds 21–22 dc (2 rnds)
Rnd 23 (dc2 into next st) 9 times (18)
Rnd 24 (dc2, dc2 into next st) 6 times (24)
Rnds 25–30 dc (6 rnds)

Rnd 31 (dc3, dc2 into next st) 6 times (30)
Rnds 32–34 dc (3 rnds)
Rnd 35 (dc4, dc2 into next st) 6 times (36)
Rnd 36 dc12, (dc1, dc2 into next st) 6 times, dc12 (42)
Rnd 37 (dc6, dc2 into next st) 6 times (48)
Rnds 38–42 dc (5 rnds)
Rnd 43 (dc6, dc2tog) 6 times (42)
Rnd 44 (dc5, dc2tog) 6 times (36)
Rnd 45 dc
Rnd 46 (dc4, dc2tog) 6 times (30)
Rnd 47 (dc3, dc2tog) 6 times (24)
Rnd 48 (dc2, dc2tog) 6 times (18)
Rnd 49 (dc2tog) 9 times (9)

ARMS (make two)
Working in Green
Ch12 and sl st to join into a circle
Rnds 1–20 dc (20 rnds)
Rnd 21 (dc5, dc2 into next st) twice (14)
Rnd 22 (dc6, dc2 into next st) twice (16)
Rnd 23 (dc7, dc2 into next st) twice (18)
Rnds 24–29 dc (6 rnds)
Continues overleaf

MADE IN Green, Pink and Oatmeal (overleaf with Hyacinth and Cream flower)
YARN QUANTITIES 50g foliage, 50g flower, 25g flower contrast
TIME TO GROW Moderate
COLOUR VARIANTS Pink, Hyacinth, Violet, Cream
REQUIRES tr

Rnd 30 (dc7, dc2tog) twice (16)
Rnd 31 (dc6, dc2tog) twice (14)
Rnd 32 (dc5, dc2tog) twice (12)
Rnd 33 (dc4, dc2tog) twice (10)
Rnd 34 (dc3, dc2tog) twice (8)
Rnd 35 (dc2, dc2tog) twice (6)
Rnd 36 (dc1, dc2tog) twice (4)
Stuff end lightly and sew flat across top to close.

LEGS (make two)
Working in Green
Ch12 and sl st to join into a circle
Rnds 1–35 dc (35 rnds)
Rnd 36 (dc2tog) 6 times (6)
Stuff foot and sew flat across top to close.

FLOWERS (make approximately 25; see chart)
Working in Pink
Begin by dc4 into ring
Rnd 1 (dc2 into next st) 4 times (8)
Rnd 2 (ch2, tr3 into next st, sl st1 into next st)
    4 times

Break yarn.

Sew flowers into position to cover head.

FLOWER CENTRES (make approximately 25)
Working in Oatmeal
Work directly onto head as follows:
sl st into position at centre of FLOWER,
    ch2, turn and dc3 into first ch.
Break yarn.

Finish by sewing eyes into place with Black and
    Cream yarn.

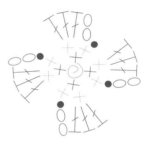

French Lavender

The colour purple is a symbol of royalty, and lavender is a flower that represents elegance, refinement and luxury. Lavender is also symbolic of health and has been celebrated for its medicinal qualities for centuries. In 17th-century London, people would tie small bunches of lavender around their wrists in the hope of avoiding infection from disease. Today, lavender extract is used in many ointments for its soothing and antibacterial properties. Due to its widely recognised fragrance, and association with relaxation and good sleep, lavender flowers can also denote purity, silence and devotion. This is the perfect 'get well soon' flower to crochet for a friend.

HEAD/BODY
Working in Sapphire
Begin by dc6 into ring
Rnd 1 (dc2 into next st) 6 times (12 sts)
Rnd 2 (dc1, dc2 into next st) 6 times (18)
Rnd 3 (dc2, dc2 into next st) 6 times (24)
Rnd 4 (dc3, dc2 into next st) 6 times (30)
Rnd 5 (dc4, dc2 into next st) 6 times (36)
Rnd 6 (dc5, dc2 into next st) 6 times (42)
Rnds 7–19 dc (13 rnds)
Rnd 20 (dc5, dc2tog) 6 times (36)
Rnd 21 (dc4, dc2tog) 6 times (30)
Rnd 22 (dc3, dc2tog) 6 times (24)
Rnd 23 (dc2, dc2tog) 6 times (18)
Rnd 24 (dc2tog) 9 times (9)
Change to Lime
Rnds 25–26 dc (2 rnds)
Rnd 27 (dc2 into next st) 9 times (18)
Rnd 28 (dc2, dc2 into next st) 6 times (24)
Rnds 29–34 dc (6 rnds)
Rnd 35 (dc3, dc2 into next st) 6 times (30)
Rnds 36–38 dc (3 rnds)

Rnd 39 (dc4, dc2 into next st) 6 times (36)
Rnd 40 dc12, (dc1, dc2 into next st) 6 times, dc12 (42)
Rnd 41 (dc6, dc2 into next st) 6 times (48)
Rnds 42–46 dc (5 rnds)
Rnd 47 (dc6, dc2tog) 6 times (42)
Rnd 48 (dc5, dc2tog) 6 times (36)
Rnd 49 dc
Rnd 50 (dc4, dc2tog) 6 times (30)
Rnd 51 (dc3, dc2tog) 6 times (24)
Rnd 52 (dc2, dc2tog) 6 times (18)
Rnd 53 (dc2tog) 9 times (9)

ARMS (make two)
Working in Lime
Ch12 and sl st to join into a circle
Rnds 1–20 dc (20 rnds)
Rnd 21 (dc5, dc2 into next st) twice (14)
Rnd 22 (dc6, dc2 into next st) twice (16)
Rnd 23 (dc7, dc2 into next st) twice (18)
Rnds 24–29 dc (6 rnds)
Continues overleaf

MADE IN Lime, Violet and Sapphire (overleaf with Magenta and Amethyst flower)
YARN QUANTITIES 50g foliage, 50g flower, 25g flower contrast
TIME TO GROW Moderate
COLOUR VARIANTS Pink, Peony, Violet, Blue, Cream
REQUIRES htr, tr, dtr

Rnd 30 (dc7, dc2tog) twice (16)
Rnd 31 (dc6, dc2tog) twice (14)
Rnd 32 (dc5, dc2tog) twice (12)
Rnd 33 (dc4, dc2tog) twice (10)
Rnd 34 (dc3, dc2tog) twice (8)
Rnd 35 (dc2, dc2tog) twice (6)
Rnd 36 (dc1, dc2tog) twice (4)
Stuff end lightly and sew flat across top to close.

LEGS (make two)
Working in Lime
Ch12 and sl st to join into a circle
Rnds 1–35 dc (35 rnds)
Rnd 36 (dc2tog) 6 times (6)
Stuff foot and sew flat across top to close.

PETALS (make five; see top chart)
Working in Violet
Sl st into top of head, ch19, turn and work back
    down chain as follows:
sl st1, dc1, htr1, tr3, dtr10, tr1, htr1, sl st back
    into head, turn and work up other side of
    ch as follows:
htr1, tr1, dtr10, tr3, htr1, dc1, sl st1
Break yarn.
Rejoin at bottom of petal and work two rnds
    of dc around edge on wrong side. Repeat
    four times.

PETAL SUPPORT
Working in Violet
Ch8 and sl st to join in a circle
Rnds 1–12 dc (12 rnds)
Sew ends together into a ring around base
of petals.

BUDS (see bottom chart)
Work four lines of four buds around head
Working in Violet
Sl st into position on neck at colour change rnd
*Ch5, sl st into head approximately 5 rnds
    up, ch5, sl st back down 1 st over from
    starting position.

Ch2, tr7 around chain into chain space, ch2,
    tr8 back down other side around chain Sl st
    back into starting stitch and break yarn.

Sl st into head through top of previous bud and
    repeat from * three more times to create a
    line of four buds up head.

Repeat three more times around head.

Finish by sewing eyes into place with Black
    and Cream yarn.

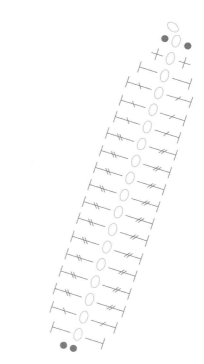

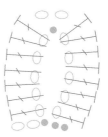

Clematis

The clematis is a very charming plant with stunning, bold flowers and an appealing range of associations. Commonly seen as representing mental strength and ingenuity, most likely stemming from its climbing habit, this plant's ability to reach seemingly limitless heights means it is associated with aspiration and used as a charm to encourage and fuel ambition. In addition, the plant's characteristic of never standing still is also reminiscent of travel and mischief. These flowers would therefore make a perfect companion for anyone with wanderlust heading off on an adventure. Due to the variety among its 300 species, it has earned lots of nicknames, including 'old man's beard', the 'climbing queen' and my favourite – the 'devil's darning needle'.

HEAD/BODY
Working in Amethyst
Begin by dc6 into ring
Rnd 1 (dc2 into next st) 6 times (12 sts)
Rnd 2 (dc1, dc2 into next st) 6 times (18)
Rnd 3 (dc2, dc2 into next st) 6 times (24)
Rnd 4 (dc3, dc2 into next st) 6 times (30)
Rnd 5 (dc4, dc2 into next st) 6 times (36)
Rnd 6 (dc5, dc2 into next st) 6 times (42)
Rnd 7 (dc6, dc2 into next st) 6 times (48)
Rnd 8 (dc7, dc2 into next st) 6 times (54)
Rnds 9–13 dc (5 rnds)
Rnd 14 (dc7, dc2tog) 6 times (48)
Rnd 15 (dc6, dc2tog) 6 times (42)
Rnd 16 (dc5, dc2tog) 6 times (36)
Rnd 17 (dc4, dc2tog) 6 times (30)
Rnd 18 (dc3, dc2tog) 6 times (24)
Rnd 19 (dc2, dc2tog) 6 times (18)
Rnd 20 (dc2tog) 9 times (9)
Change to Lime
Rnds 21–22 dc (2 rnds)

Rnd 23 (dc2 into next st) 9 times (18)
Rnd 24 (dc2, dc2 into next st) 6 times (24)
Rnds 25–30 dc (6 rnds)
Rnd 31 (dc3, dc2 into next st) 6 times (30)
Rnds 32–34 dc (3 rnds)
Rnd 35 (dc4, dc2 into next st) 6 times (36)
Rnd 36 dc12, (dc1, dc2 into next st) 6 times, dc12 (42)
Rnd 37 (dc6, dc2 into next st) 6 times (48)
Rnds 38–42 dc (5 rnds)
Rnd 43 (dc6, dc2tog) 6 times (42)
Rnd 44 (dc5, dc2tog) 6 times (36)
Rnd 45 dc
Rnd 46 (dc4, dc2tog) 6 times (30)
Rnd 47 (dc3, dc2tog) 6 times (24)
Rnd 48 (dc2, dc2tog) 6 times (18)
Rnd 49 (dc2tog) 9 times (9)

ARMS (make two)
Working in Lime
Continues overleaf

MADE IN Lime, Cream and Amethyst
YARN QUANTITIES 50g foliage, 50g flower, 25g flower contrast
TIME TO GROW Moderate
COLOUR VARIANTS Violet
REQUIRES Slip stitch traverse

Ch12 and sl st to join into a circle
Rnds 1–20 dc (20 rnds)
Rnd 21 (dc5, dc2 into next st) twice (14)
Rnd 22 (dc6, dc2 into next st) twice (16)
Rnd 23 (dc7, dc2 into next st) twice (18)
Rnds 24–29 dc (6 rnds)
Rnd 30 (dc7, dc2tog) twice (16)
Rnd 31 (dc6, dc2tog) twice (14)
Rnd 32 (dc5, dc2tog) twice (12)
Rnd 33 (dc4, dc2tog) twice (10)
Rnd 34 (dc3, dc2tog) twice (8)
Rnd 35 (dc2, dc2tog) twice (6)
Rnd 36 (dc1, dc2tog) twice (4)
Stuff end lightly and sew flat across top to close.

LEGS (make two)
Working in Lime
Ch12 and sl st to join into a circle
Rnds 1–35 dc (35 rnds)
Rnd 36 (dc2tog) 6 times (6)
Stuff foot and sew flat across top to close.

PETALS (make six)
Working in Cream
Ch24 and sl st to join in a circle
Rnd 1 dc
Rnd 2 (dc3, dc2 into next st) 6 times (30)
Rnd 3 (dc4, dc2 into next st) 6 times (36)
Rnds 4–6 dc (3 rnds)
Rnd 7 (dc2tog, dc10) 3 times (33)
Rnd 8 (dc2tog, dc9) 3 times (30)

Rnd 9 (dc2tog, dc8) 3 times (27)
Rnd 10 (dc2tog, dc7) 3 times (24)
Rnd 11 (dc2tog, dc6) 3 times (21)
Rnd 12 (dc2tog, dc5) 3 times (18)
Rnd 13 (dc2tog, dc4) 3 times (15)
Rnd 14 (dc2tog, dc3) 3 times (12)
Rnd 15 (dc2tog, dc2) 3 times (9)
Break yarn.

Make two rings of petals by dc along bottom
    of each petal with ch4 between each petal.
Sew into position on head (see pages 152–153).

INNER PETALS
Working in Amethyst
Work a round of INNER PETALS in front of the
    PETALS (approximately 18)
Sl st into position, *ch6, turn and work back
    down chain as follows:
sl st1, dc1, htr3
Miss approximately 2 sts along head, sl st and
    repeat from *.

Working in Lime
SLIP STITCH TRAVERSE (see page 154) a rnd of
    sts in front of the previous INNER PETALS.

Finish by sewing eyes into place with Black and
    Cream yarn.

Poppy

Of all the flowers in this book, few have played such an important role in religion, mythology, politics and medicine as the poppy. Poppies are considered a symbol of both sleep and death, due to their opiate qualities. The sight of these flowers in the destroyed landscape of the Western Front after World War I has made them representative of the blood of fallen soldiers, and they are widely recognised as an emblem of remembrance. With over 70 species now available, they are particularly beautiful in Cream and Pink, in addition to the iconic Ruby. White poppies go beyond the theme of remembrance, providing a symbol of peace and pacifism.

HEAD/BODY

Working in Cocoa
Begin by dc6 into ring
Rnd 1 (dc2 into next st) 6 times (12 sts)
Rnd 2 (dc1, dc2 into next st) 6 times (18)
Rnd 3 (dc2, dc2 into next st) 6 times (24)
Rnd 4 (dc3, dc2 into next st) 6 times (30)
Rnd 5 (dc4, dc2 into next st) 6 times (36)
Rnd 6 (dc5, dc2 into next st) 6 times (42)
Rnd 7 (dc6, dc2 into next st) 6 times (48)
Rnd 8 (dc7, dc2 into next st) 6 times (54)
Rnds 9–13 dc (5 rnds)
Rnd 14 (dc7, dc2tog) 6 times (48)
Rnd 15 (dc6, dc2tog) 6 times (42)
Rnd 16 (dc5, dc2tog) 6 times (36)
Rnd 17 (dc4, dc2tog) 6 times (30)
Rnd 18 (dc3, dc2tog) 6 times (24)
Rnd 19 (dc2, dc2tog) 6 times (18)
Rnd 20 (dc2tog) 9 times (9)
Change to Green
Rnds 21–22 dc (2 rnds)
Rnd 23 (dc2 into next st) 9 times (18)
Rnd 24 (dc2, dc2 into next st) 6 times (24)

Rnds 25–30 dc (6 rnds)
Rnd 31 (dc3, dc2 into next st) 6 times (30)
Rnds 32–34 dc (3 rnds)
Rnd 35 (dc4, dc2 into next st) 6 times (36)
Rnd 36 dc12, (dc1, dc2 into next st) 6 times, dc12 (42)
Rnd 37 (dc6, dc2 into next st) 6 times (48)
Rnds 38–42 dc (5 rnds)
Rnd 43 (dc6, dc2tog) 6 times (42)
Rnd 44 (dc5, dc2tog) 6 times (36)
Rnd 45 dc
Rnd 46 (dc4, dc2tog) 6 times (30)
Rnd 47 (dc3, dc2tog) 6 times (24)
Rnd 48 (dc2, dc2tog) 6 times (18)
Rnd 49 (dc2tog) 9 times (9)

ARMS (make two)

Working in Green
Ch12 and sl st to join into a circle
Rnds 1–20 dc (20 rnds)
Rnd 21 (dc5, dc2 into next st) twice (14)
Rnd 22 (dc6, dc2 into next st) twice (16)
Continues overleaf

MADE IN Green, Cream and Cocoa (overleaf with Ruby and Black flower)
YARN QUANTITIES 50g foliage, 50g flower, 25g flower contrast
TIME TO GROW Moderate
COLOUR VARIANTS Orange, Pink, Peony, Cream
REQUIRES Just the basics!

Rnd 23 (dc7, dc2 into next st) twice (18)
Rnds 24–29 dc (6 rnds)
Rnd 30 (dc7, dc2tog) twice (16)
Rnd 31 (dc6, dc2tog) twice (14)
Rnd 32 (dc5, dc2tog) twice (12)
Rnd 33 (dc4, dc2tog) twice (10)
Rnd 34 (dc3, dc2tog) twice (8)
Rnd 35 (dc2, dc2tog) twice (6)
Rnd 36 (dc1, dc2tog) twice (4)
Stuff end lightly and sew flat across top to close.

LEGS (make two)
Working in Green
Ch12 and sl st to join into a circle
Rnds 1–35 dc (35 rnds)
Rnd 36 (dc2tog) 6 times (6)
Stuff foot and sew flat across top to close.

PETALS (make four)
Working in Cream
Begin by dc6 into ring

Rnd 1 (dc2 into next st) 6 times (12)
Rnd 2 (dc1, dc2 into next st) 6 times (18)
Rnd 3 (dc2, dc2 into next st) 6 times (24)
Rnd 4 (dc3, dc2 into next st) 6 times (30)
Rnd 5 (dc4, dc2 into next st) 6 times (36)
Rnd 6 dc
Rnd 7 (dc5, dc2 into next st) 6 times (42)
Rnd 8 (dc6, dc2 into next st) 6 times (48)
Rnds 9–11 dc (3 rnds)
Rnd 12 (dc6, dc2tog) 6 times (42)
Rnds 13–16 dc (4 rnds)
Rnd 17 (dc5, dc2tog) 6 times (36)
Dc across to bottom of petal to close.

Make two rings of petals by dc along bottom of
    each petal with ch3 between each petal.
Sew into position on head (see pages 152–153).

Finish by sewing eyes into place with Black and
    Cream yarn.

Foxglove

Foxgloves have held many symbolic meanings, both positive and negative. The flowers have been associated with insincerity, pride, intuition, creativity and energy. In the Victorian language of flowers, a gift of foxgloves meant 'I am ambitious for you, rather than for myself.' In Europe, the foxglove is commonly known as 'fairy's gloves' or 'fairy thimbles'. It was once thought that the disturbed soil in which foxgloves prefer to grow was, perhaps, the territory of the little folk. Hence, some believe that the flowers were once called 'folk's glove', which eventually changed into foxglove.

HEAD/BODY
Working in Lime
Begin by dc6 into ring
Rnd 1 (dc2 into next st) 6 times (12 sts)
Rnd 2 (dc1, dc2 into next st) 6 times (18)
Rnd 3 (dc2, dc2 into next st) 6 times (24)
Rnd 4 (dc3, dc2 into next st) 6 times (30)
Rnd 5 (dc4, dc2 into next st) 6 times (36)
Rnd 6 (dc5, dc2 into next st) 6 times (42)
Rnds 7–19 dc (13 rnds)
Rnd 20 (dc5, dc2tog) 6 times (36)
Rnd 21 (dc4, dc2tog) 6 times (30)
Rnd 22 (dc3, dc2tog) 6 times (24)
Rnd 23 (dc2, dc2tog) 6 times (18)
Rnd 24 (dc2tog) 9 times (9)
Change to Green
Rnds 25–26 dc (2 rnds)
Rnd 27 (dc2 into next st) 9 times (18)
Rnd 28 (dc2, dc2 into next st) 6 times (24)
Rnds 29–34 dc (6 rnds)
Rnd 35 (dc3, dc2 into next st) 6 times (30)
Rnds 36–38 dc (3 rnds)
Rnd 39 (dc4, dc2 into next st) 6 times (36)

Rnd 40 dc12, (dc1, dc2 into next st) 6 times, dc12 (42)
Rnd 41 (dc6, dc2 into next st) 6 times (48)
Rnds 42–46 dc (5 rnds)
Rnd 47 (dc6, dc2tog) 6 times (42)
Rnd 48 (dc5, dc2tog) 6 times (36)
Rnd 49 dc
Rnd 50 (dc4, dc2tog) 6 times (30)
Rnd 51 (dc3, dc2tog) 6 times (24)
Rnd 52 (dc2, dc2tog) 6 times (18)
Rnd 53 (dc2tog) 9 times (9)

ARMS (make two)
Working in Green
Ch12 and sl st to join into a circle
Rnds 1–20 dc (20 rnds)
Rnd 21 (dc5, dc2 into next st) twice (14)
Rnd 22 (dc6, dc2 into next st) twice (16)
Rnd 23 (dc7, dc2 into next st) twice (18)
Rnds 24–29 dc (6 rnds)
Rnd 30 (dc7, dc2tog) twice (16)
Rnd 31 (dc6, dc2tog) twice (14)
Continues overleaf

MADE IN Green, Lime and Peony (overleaf with Magenta flowers)
YARN QUANTITIES 50g foliage, 25g foliage contrast, 50g flowers
TIME TO GROW Slow grower
COLOUR VARIANTS Pink, Magenta, Cream, Coral, Primrose
REQUIRES htr, tr

Rnd 32 (dc5, dc2tog) twice (12)
Rnd 33 (dc4, dc2tog) twice (10)
Rnd 34 (dc3, dc2tog) twice (8)
Rnd 35 (dc2, dc2tog) twice (6)
Rnd 36 (dc1, dc2tog) twice (4)
Stuff end lightly and sew flat across top to close.

LEGS (make two)
Working in Green
Ch12 and sl st to join into a circle
Rnds 1–35 dc (35 rnds)
Rnd 36 (dc2tog) 6 times (6)
Stuff foot and sew flat across top to close.

SMALL FLOWERS (make 12)
Working in Lime
Begin by dc6 into ring
Rnds 1–2 dc (2 rnds)
Change to Peony
Rnd 3 (dc2 into next st) 6 times (12)
Break yarn.

MEDIUM FLOWERS (make 18)
Working in Peony
Begin by dc6 into ring
Rnd 1 (dc1, dc2 into next st) 3 times (9)
Rnds 2–5 dc (4 rnds)
Rnd 6 (dc2 into next st) 9 times (18)

Rnd 7 dc2, htr2, dc2 (incomplete rnd)
Break yarn.

LARGE FLOWERS (make 12)
Working in Peony
Begin by dc6 into ring
Rnd 1 (dc2 into next st) 6 times (12)
Rnds 2–6 dc (5 rnds)
Rnd 7 (dc2 into next st) 12 times (24)
Rnd 8 dc2, htr2, tr3, htr2, dc15
Break yarn.

Work 6 vertical lines of flowers onto head in
    the following order from bottom up:
2 LARGE, 3 MEDIUM, 2 SMALL

Working in Lime
Sl st through starting ring of flower and
    into head at neck, *ch3, sl st into head
    approximately 4 rnds up, sl st into next
    flower and repeat from * to create a line
    of seven petals.

Repeat five more times around the head. See
    Heather, page 53, for illustration.

Finish by sewing eyes into place with Black and
    Cream yarn.

Sunflower

One of the easiest flowers to plant from seed, and a fantastic place to start for any budding young gardeners who would like to create a real garden. Many people view sunflowers as highly spiritual symbols of unswerving faith, loyalty, dedicated love, devotion and adoration. This flower represents happiness, radiance and all things positive, so it makes a brilliant good luck charm for anyone who needs a radiant boost of positivity in their life.

HEAD/BODY
Working in Chestnut
Begin by dc6 into ring
Rnd 1 (dc2 into next st) 6 times (12 sts)
Rnd 2 (dc1, dc2 into next st) 6 times (18)
Rnd 3 (dc2, dc2 into next st) 6 times (24)
Rnd 4 (dc3, dc2 into next st) 6 times (30)
Rnd 5 (dc4, dc2 into next st) 6 times (36)
Rnd 6 (dc5, dc2 into next st) 6 times (42)
Rnd 7 (dc6, dc2 into next st) 6 times (48)
Rnd 8 (dc7, dc2 into next st) 6 times (54)
Rnds 9–13 dc (5 rnds)
Rnd 14 (dc7, dc2tog) 6 times (48)
Rnd 15 (dc6, dc2tog) 6 times (42)
Rnd 16 (dc5, dc2tog) 6 times (36)
Rnd 17 (dc4, dc2tog) 6 times (30)
Rnd 18 (dc3, dc2tog) 6 times (24)
Rnd 19 (dc2, dc2tog) 6 times (18)
Rnd 20 (dc2tog) 9 times (9)
Change to Green
Rnds 21–22 dc (2 rnds)
Rnd 23 (dc2 into next st) 9 times (18)
Rnd 24 (dc2, dc2 into next st) 6 times (24)
Rnds 25–30 dc (6 rnds)
Rnd 31 (dc3, dc2 into next st) 6 times (30)

Rnds 32–34 dc (3 rnds)
Rnd 35 (dc4, dc2 into next st) 6 times (36)
Rnd 36 dc12, (dc1, dc2 into next st) 6 times, dc12 (42)
Rnd 37 (dc6, dc2 into next st) 6 times (48)
Rnds 38–42 dc (5 rnds)
Rnd 43 (dc6, dc2tog) 6 times (42)
Rnd 44 (dc5, dc2tog) 6 times (36)
Rnd 45 dc
Rnd 46 (dc4, dc2tog) 6 times (30)
Rnd 47 (dc3, dc2tog) 6 times (24)
Rnd 48 (dc2, dc2tog) 6 times (18)
Rnd 49 (dc2tog) 9 times (9)

ARMS (make two)
Working in Green
Ch12 and sl st to join into a circle
Rnds 1–20 dc (20 rnds)
Rnd 21 (dc5, dc2 into next st) twice (14)
Rnd 22 (dc6, dc2 into next st) twice (16)
Rnd 23 (dc7, dc2 into next st) twice (18)
Rnds 24–29 dc (6 rnds)
Rnd 30 (dc7, dc2tog) twice (16)
Rnd 31 (dc6, dc2tog) twice (14)
Continues overleaf

MADE IN Green, Yellow and Chestnut
YARN QUANTITIES 50g foliage, 50g flower, 25g flower contrast
TIME TO GROW Slow grower
COLOUR VARIANTS Primrose, Orange and Ruby
REQUIRES Just the basics!

Rnd 32 (dc5, dc2tog) twice (12)
Rnd 33 (dc4, dc2tog) twice (10)
Rnd 34 (dc3, dc2tog) twice (8)
Rnd 35 (dc2, dc2tog) twice (6)
Rnd 36 (dc1, dc2tog) twice (4)
Stuff end lightly and sew flat across top to close.

LEGS (make two)
Working in Green
Ch12 and sl st to join into a circle
Rnds 1–35 dc (35 rnds)
Rnd 36 (dc2tog) 6 times (6)
Stuff foot and sew flat across top to close.

PETALS (make 28)
Working in Yellow

Begin by dc6 into ring
Rnds 1–2 dc (2 rnds)
Rnd 3 (dc2 into next st, dc2) twice (8)
Rnds 4–6 dc (3 rnds)
Rnd 7 (dc2, dc2tog) twice (6)
Rnd 8 (dc1, dc2tog) twice (4)

Working in Yellow
Make a ring of 14 petals by dc3 along bottom
    of each petal to join together.
Repeat to make a second ring of 14 petals and
    then sew both into position on head with
    one in front of the other (see pages 152–153).

Finish by sewing eyes into place with Black and
    Cream yarn.

Gerbera

The gerbera daisy has different meanings in different cultures but it is generally associated with happiness and comfort. The Ancient Egyptians believed that it symbolised a closeness to nature, whereas the Celts thought it lessened the sorrows and stresses of everyday life. Generally, gerberas stand for cheerfulness and loyal love. Orange gerberas can signify euphoria, laughter and platonic love. These flowers, especially in yellow and orange, make an excellent gift for the friends who make you laugh the most, or to bring happiness to a loved one in need of a smile.

HEAD/BODY
Working in Fudge
Begin by dc6 into ring
Rnd 1 (dc2 into next st) 6 times (12 sts)
Rnd 2 (dc1, dc2 into next st) 6 times (18)
Rnd 3 (dc2, dc2 into next st) 6 times (24)
Rnd 4 (dc3, dc2 into next st) 6 times (30)
Rnd 5 (dc4, dc2 into next st) 6 times (36)
Rnd 6 (dc5, dc2 into next st) 6 times (42)
Rnd 7 (dc6, dc2 into next st) 6 times (48)
Rnd 8 (dc7, dc2 into next st) 6 times (54)
Rnds 9–13 dc (5 rnds)
Rnd 14 (dc7, dc2tog) 6 times (48)
Rnd 15 (dc6, dc2tog) 6 times (42)
Rnd 16 (dc5, dc2tog) 6 times (36)
Rnd 17 (dc4, dc2tog) 6 times (30)
Rnd 18 (dc3, dc2tog) 6 times (24)
Rnd 19 (dc2, dc2tog) 6 times (18)
Rnd 20 (dc2tog) 9 times (9)
Change to Lime
Rnds 21–22 dc (2 rnds)
Rnd 23 (dc2 into next st) 9 times (18)
Rnd 24 (dc2, dc2 into next st) 6 times (24)

Rnds 25–30 dc (6 rnds)
Rnd 31 (dc3, dc2 into next st) 6 times (30)
Rnds 32–34 dc (3 rnds)
Rnd 35 (dc4, dc2 into next st) 6 times (36)
Rnd 36 dc12, (dc1, dc2 into next st) 6 times, dc12 (42)
Rnd 37 (dc6, dc2 into next st) 6 times (48)
Rnds 38–42 dc (5 rnds)
Rnd 43 (dc6, dc2tog) 6 times (42)
Rnd 44 (dc5, dc2tog) 6 times (36)
Rnd 45 dc
Rnd 46 (dc4, dc2tog) 6 times (30)
Rnd 47 (dc3, dc2tog) 6 times (24)
Rnd 48 (dc2, dc2tog) 6 times (18)
Rnd 49 (dc2tog) 9 times (9)

ARMS (make two)
Working in Lime
Ch12 and sl st to join into a circle
Rnds 1–20 dc (20 rnds)
Rnd 21 (dc5, dc2 into next st) twice (14)
Rnd 22 (dc6, dc2 into next st) twice (16)
Continues overleaf

MADE IN Lime, Orange and Fudge (overleaf with Magenta and Mushroom flower)
YARN QUANTITIES 50g foliage, 50g flower, 25g flower contrast
TIME TO GROW Slow grower
COLOUR VARIANTS Pink, Yellow, Orange, Amethyst, Cream
REQUIRES Slip stitch chain, slip stitch traverse

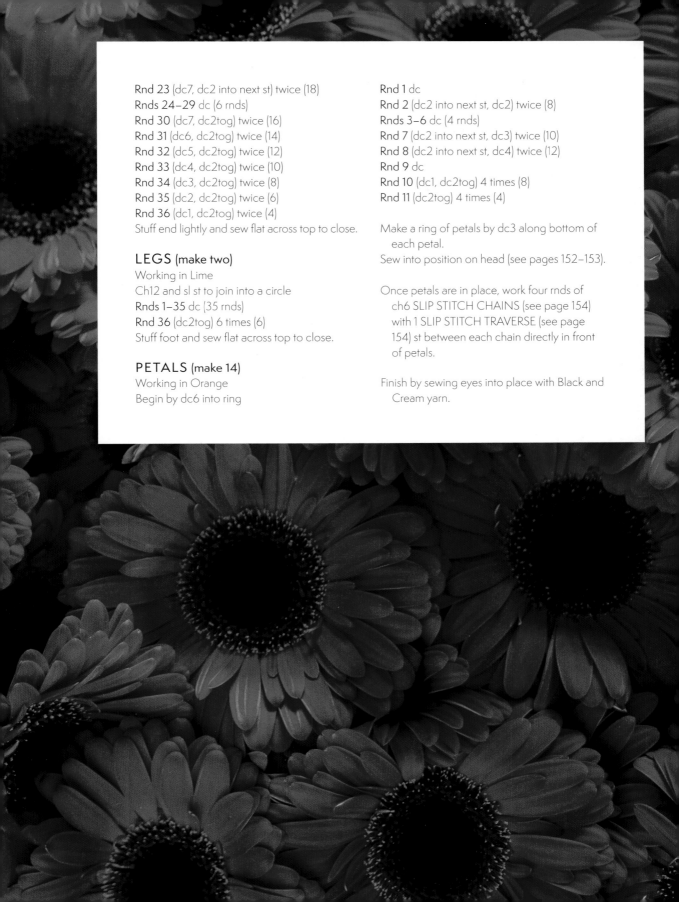

Rnd 23 (dc7, dc2 into next st) twice (18)
Rnds 24–29 dc (6 rnds)
Rnd 30 (dc7, dc2tog) twice (16)
Rnd 31 (dc6, dc2tog) twice (14)
Rnd 32 (dc5, dc2tog) twice (12)
Rnd 33 (dc4, dc2tog) twice (10)
Rnd 34 (dc3, dc2tog) twice (8)
Rnd 35 (dc2, dc2tog) twice (6)
Rnd 36 (dc1, dc2tog) twice (4)
Stuff end lightly and sew flat across top to close.

LEGS (make two)
Working in Lime
Ch12 and sl st to join into a circle
Rnds 1–35 dc (35 rnds)
Rnd 36 (dc2tog) 6 times (6)
Stuff foot and sew flat across top to close.

PETALS (make 14)
Working in Orange
Begin by dc6 into ring

Rnd 1 dc
Rnd 2 (dc2 into next st, dc2) twice (8)
Rnds 3–6 dc (4 rnds)
Rnd 7 (dc2 into next st, dc3) twice (10)
Rnd 8 (dc2 into next st, dc4) twice (12)
Rnd 9 dc
Rnd 10 (dc1, dc2tog) 4 times (8)
Rnd 11 (dc2tog) 4 times (4)

Make a ring of petals by dc3 along bottom of each petal.
Sew into position on head (see pages 152–153).

Once petals are in place, work four rnds of ch6 SLIP STITCH CHAINS (see page 154) with 1 SLIP STITCH TRAVERSE (see page 154) st between each chain directly in front of petals.

Finish by sewing eyes into place with Black and Cream yarn.

Marigold

Marigolds are flowers with huge cultural significance, used in religious ceremonies dating back to the Aztecs through to the temples of modern India. Symbols of positive energy, warmth, joy and happiness, they are used to encourage optimism, hope and good fortune. The colours of the sun, they come in every shade of yellow, copper, rust and gold and are commonly referred to as the 'herb of the sun', thought to embody the light within us. Many cultures also associate marigolds with honouring the dead and remembrance of lost loved ones, and they have also come to symbolise a lost love, whether through death or a broken relationship.

HEAD/BODY
Working in Orange
Begin by dc6 into ring
Rnd 1 (dc2 into next st) 6 times (12 sts)
Rnd 2 (dc1, dc2 into next st) 6 times (18)
Rnd 3 (dc2, dc2 into next st) 6 times (24)
Rnd 4 (dc3, dc2 into next st) 6 times (30)
Rnd 5 (dc4, dc2 into next st) 6 times (36)
Rnd 6 (dc5, dc2 into next st) 6 times (42)
Rnd 7 (dc6, dc2 into next st) 6 times (48)
Rnd 8 (dc7, dc2 into next st) 6 times (54)
Rnds 9–13 dc (5 rnds)
Rnd 14 (dc7, dc2tog) 6 times (48)
Rnd 15 (dc6, dc2tog) 6 times (42)
Rnd 16 (dc5, dc2tog) 6 times (36)
Rnd 17 (dc4, dc2tog) 6 times (30)
Rnd 18 (dc3, dc2tog) 6 times (24)
Rnd 19 (dc2, dc2tog) 6 times (18)
Rnd 20 (dc2tog) 9 times (9)
Change to Green
Rnds 21–22 dc (2 rnds)
Rnd 23 (dc2 into next st) 9 times (18)

Rnd 24 (dc2, dc2 into next st) 6 times (24)
Rnds 25–30 dc (6 rnds)
Rnd 31 (dc3, dc2 into next st) 6 times (30)
Rnds 32–34 dc (3 rnds)
Rnd 35 (dc4, dc2 into next st) 6 times (36)
Rnd 36 dc12, (dc1, dc2 into next st) 6 times, dc12 (42)
Rnd 37 (dc6, dc2 into next st) 6 times (48)
Rnds 38–42 dc (5 rnds)
Rnd 43 (dc6, dc2tog) 6 times (42)
Rnd 44 (dc5, dc2tog) 6 times (36)
Rnd 45 dc
Rnd 46 (dc4, dc2tog) 6 times (30)
Rnd 47 (dc3, dc2tog) 6 times (24)
Rnd 48 (dc2, dc2tog) 6 times (18)
Rnd 49 (dc2tog) 9 times (9)

ARMS (make two)
Working in Green
Ch12 and sl st to join into a circle
Rnds 1–20 dc (20 rnds)
Continues overleaf

MADE IN Green, Yellow and Orange
YARN QUANTITIES 50g foliage, 50g flower, 25g flower contrast
TIME TO GROW Moderate
COLOUR VARIANTS Yellow, Ruby, Cream, Coral, Primrose
REQUIRES Slip stitch traverse

Rnd 21 (dc5, dc2 into next st) twice (14)
Rnd 22 (dc6, dc2 into next st) twice (16)
Rnd 23 (dc7, dc2 into next st) twice (18)
Rnds 24–29 dc (6 rnds)
Rnd 30 (dc7, dc2tog) twice (16)
Rnd 31 (dc6, dc2tog) twice (14)
Rnd 32 (dc5, dc2tog) twice (12)
Rnd 33 (dc4, dc2tog) twice (10)
Rnd 34 (dc3, dc2tog) twice (8)
Rnd 35 (dc2, dc2tog) twice (6)
Rnd 36 (dc1, dc2tog) twice (4)
Stuff end lightly and sew flat across top to close.

LEGS (make two)
Working in Green
Ch12 and sl st to join into a circle
Rnds 1–35 dc (35 rnds)
Rnd 36 (dc2tog) 6 times (6)
Stuff foot and sew flat across top to close.

BLOOMS
Working in Orange
Row 1 Starting from the centre on top of head, SLIP STITCH TRAVERSE (see page 154) in a spiral outwards and downwards around head.
Row 2 Once you reach edge of head, ch1, turn, then dc2 into every st back along spiral to return to centre of head.
Row 3 Ch1, turn and (dc1, dc2 into next st) back along spiral.
Change to Yellow.
Row 4 Dc1 into every st around bottom circle of spiral. Break yarn. *Miss 12 sts of Orange and dc8 sts in Yellow. Repeat from * to centre top of head.

Finish by sewing eyes into place with Black and Cream yarn.

Dahlia

The meaning of these flowers depends on your relationship to the person you give them to, and those meanings are as varied as the shape and forms of dahlias themselves. Given to a lover, the dahlia means 'forever thine' – a deep symbol of a lasting bond and lifelong commitment. Generally speaking, these late Summer-blooming flowers symbolise inner strength, change, creativity and dignity. Other meanings include remaining graceful and standing out from the crowd, since the dahlia's bold beauty is second to none in the flowerbed. For the Aztecs, the dahlia was a religious symbol and also used for medicine and food (you can eat the tubers!) in addition to having an important role in ceremonies.

HEAD/BODY
Working in Coral
Begin by dc6 into ring
Rnd 1 (dc2 into next st) 6 times (12 sts)
Rnd 2 (dc1, dc2 into next st) 6 times (18)
Rnd 3 (dc2, dc2 into next st) 6 times (24)
Rnd 4 (dc3, dc2 into next st) 6 times (30)
Rnd 5 (dc4, dc2 into next st) 6 times (36)
Rnd 6 (dc5, dc2 into next st) 6 times (42)
Rnd 7 (dc6, dc2 into next st) 6 times (48)
Rnd 8 (dc7, dc2 into next st) 6 times (54)
Rnds 9–13 dc (5 rnds)
Rnd 14 (dc7, dc2tog) 6 times (48)
Rnd 15 (dc6, dc2tog) 6 times (42)
Rnd 16 (dc5, dc2tog) 6 times (36)
Rnd 17 (dc4, dc2tog) 6 times (30)
Rnd 18 (dc3, dc2tog) 6 times (24)
Rnd 19 (dc2, dc2tog) 6 times (18)
Rnd 20 (dc2tog) 9 times (9)
Change to Green
Rnds 21–22 dc (2 rnds)
Rnd 23 (dc2 into next st) 9 times (18)

Rnd 24 (dc2, dc2 into next st) 6 times (24)
Rnds 25–30 dc (6 rnds)
Rnd 31 (dc3, dc2 into next st) 6 times (30)
Rnds 32–34 dc (3 rnds)
Rnd 35 (dc4, dc2 into next st) 6 times (36)
Rnd 36 dc12, (dc1, dc2 into next st) 6 times, dc12 (42)
Rnd 37 (dc6, dc2 into next st) 6 times (48)
Rnds 38–42 dc (5 rnds)
Rnd 43 (dc6, dc2tog) 6 times (42)
Rnd 44 (dc5, dc2tog) 6 times (36)
Rnd 45 dc
Rnd 46 (dc4, dc2tog) 6 times (30)
Rnd 47 (dc3, dc2tog) 6 times (24)
Rnd 48 (dc2, dc2tog) 6 times (18)
Rnd 49 (dc2tog) 9 times (9)

ARMS (make two)
Working in Green
Ch12 and sl st to join into a circle
Rnds 1–20 dc (20 rnds)
Continues overleaf

MADE IN Green and Coral (overleaf with Magenta flower)
YARN QUANTITIES 50g foliage, 75g flower
TIME TO GROW Moderate
COLOUR VARIANTS Yellow, Ruby, Cream
REQUIRES htr, tr

Rnd 21 (dc5, dc2 into next st) twice (14)
Rnd 22 (dc6, dc2 into next st) twice (16)
Rnd 23 (dc7, dc2 into next st) twice (18)
Rnds 24–29 dc (6 rnds)
Rnd 30 (dc7, dc2tog) twice (16)
Rnd 31 (dc6, dc2tog) twice (14)
Rnd 32 (dc5, dc2tog) twice (12)
Rnd 33 (dc4, dc2tog) twice (10)
Rnd 34 (dc3, dc2tog) twice (8)
Rnd 35 (dc2, dc2tog) twice (6)
Rnd 36 (dc1, dc2tog) twice (4)
Stuff end lightly and sew flat across top to close.

LEGS (make two)
Working in Green
Ch12 and sl st to join into a circle
Rnds 1–35 dc (35 rnds)
Rnd 36 (dc2tog) 6 times (6)
Stuff foot and sew flat across top to close.

PETALS (make nine)
Working in Coral
Ch22, turn and work back down chain as follows:
(dc2 into next st) 3 times, (htr2 into next st)
    3 times, (tr2 into next st) 3 times, dc12

Count back 12 sts and join these sts into
    a 12-st round
Rnd 1 dc (12)
Rnd 2 (dc5, dc2 into next st) twice (14)
Rnd 3 (dc6, dc2 into next st) twice (16)
Rnd 4 (dc7, dc2 into next st) twice (18)
Rnds 5–11 dc (7 rnds)
Rnd 12 (dc7, dc2tog) twice (16)
Rnd 13 (dc6, dc2tog) twice (14)
Rnd 14 (dc5, dc2tog) twice (12)
Rnd 15 (dc4, dc2tog) twice (10)
Rnd 16 (dc3, dc2tog) twice (8)
Rnd 17 (dc2, dc2tog) twice (6)
Rnd 18 (dc1, dc2tog) twice (4)
Dc5 across bottom of first petal to close and
    tack down end of spiral at the same time.

Make a ring of petals by dc5 sts along bottom
    of each petal.
Sew into position on head (see pages 152–153).

Finish by sewing eyes into place with Black and
    Cream yarn.

Echinacea

The echinacea, or 'purple cone flower', is a symbol of strength and healing and has a long history in folklore, medicine and ritual tradition. It has often been connected with the shadowy side of spirituality and is frequently used in witchcraft to enhance the power of any spell cast. It is believed that carrying this flower will strengthen your spirit in turbulent times. It also keeps very well as a dried flower. The name echinacea comes from the Latin *ekhinos*, meaning 'hedgehog', referring to the spiky centre. To make this flower, we use a stitch with a loop, not used elsewhere in the book.

HEAD/BODY
Working in Fudge
Work 1cm LOOP STITCH (see page 149) every
　other st on every other rnd
Begin by dc6 into ring
Rnd 1 (dc2 into next st) 6 times (12 sts)
Rnd 2 dc
Rnd 3 (dc1, dc2 into next st) 6 times (18)
Rnd 4 dc
Rnd 5 (dc2, dc2 into next st) 6 times (24)
Rnd 6 dc
Rnd 7 (dc3, dc2 into next st) 6 times (30)
Rnd 8 dc
Rnd 9 (dc4, dc2 into next st) 6 times (36)
Rnd 10 (dc5, dc2 into next st) 6 times (42)
Rnd 11 (dc6, dc2 into next st) 6 times (48)
Rnd 12 (dc7, dc2 into next st) 6 times (54)
Rnds 13–17 dc (5 rnds)
Rnd 18 (dc7, dc2tog) 6 times (48)
Continue without loops
Rnd 19 (dc6, dc2tog) 6 times (42)
Rnd 20 (dc5, dc2tog) 6 times (36)
Rnd 21 (dc4, dc2tog) 6 times (30)

Rnd 22 (dc3, dc2tog) 6 times (24)
Rnd 23 (dc2, dc2tog) 6 times (18)
Rnd 24 (dc2tog) 9 times (9)
Change to Green
Rnds 25–26 dc (2 rnds)
Rnd 27 (dc2 into next st) 9 times (18)
Rnd 28 (dc2, dc2 into next st) 6 times (24)
Rnds 29–34 dc (6 rnds)
Rnd 35 (dc3, dc2 into next st) 6 times (30)
Rnds 36–38 dc (3 rnds)
Rnd 39 (dc4, dc2 into next st) 6 times (36)
Rnd 40 dc12, (dc1, dc2 into next st) 6 times,
　dc12 (42)
Rnd 41 (dc6, dc2 into next st) 6 times (48)
Rnds 42–46 dc (5 rnds)
Rnd 47 (dc6, dc2tog) 6 times (42)
Rnd 48 (dc5, dc2tog) 6 times (36)
Rnd 49 dc
Rnd 50 (dc4, dc2tog) 6 times (30)
Rnd 51 (dc3, dc2tog) 6 times (24)
Rnd 52 (dc2, dc2tog) 6 times (18)
Rnd 53 (dc2tog) 9 times (9)
Continues overleaf

MADE IN Green, Fudge and Magenta (see overleaf with Cream petals and Camel head)
YARN QUANTITIES 50g foliage, 50g flower, 25g flower contrast
TIME TO GROW Slow grower
COLOUR VARIANTS Pink, Peony, Cream
REQUIRES tr, dtr, ttr, loop stitch

ARMS (make two)

Working in Green

Ch12 and sl st to join into a circle

Rnds 1–20 dc (20 rnds)

Rnd 21 (dc5, dc2 into next st) twice (14)

Rnd 22 (dc6, dc2 into next st) twice (16)

Rnd 23 (dc7, dc2 into next st) twice (18)

Rnds 24–29 dc (6 rnds)

Rnd 30 (dc7, dc2tog) twice (16)

Rnd 31 (dc6, dc2tog) twice (14)

Rnd 32 (dc5, dc2tog) twice (12)

Rnd 33 (dc4, dc2tog) twice (10)

Rnd 34 (dc3, dc2tog) twice (8)

Rnd 35 (dc2, dc2tog) twice (6)

Rnd 36 (dc1, dc2tog) twice (4)

Stuff end lightly and sew flat across top to close.

LEGS (make two)

Working in Green

Ch12 and sl st to join into a circle

Rnds 1–35 dc (35 rnds)

Rnd 36 (dc2tog) 6 times (6)

Stuff foot and sew flat across top to close.

PETALS (make seven)

Working in Magenta

Ch26, turn and work back down chain
    as follows:

miss 2, dtr6, ttr17, ttr6 into next st

Turn and work down other side of chain
    as follows:

ttr17, dtr6

Work a rnd of dc around edge of each petal.

Make a ring of petals by dc7 along bottom of
    each petal.

Sew into position on head (see pages 152–153).

Finish by cutting loops and sewing eyes into
    place with Black and Cream yarn.

LOOP STITCH

1 Insert the hook through the stitch. Wrap the yarn from front to back over the thumb of your non-hook hand and yarn over with the yarn behind your thumb.

2 Hold the loop on your thumb and complete the double crochet stitch.

3 Moving your thumb forwards, release the loop to position it on the right side of the fabric. Work the next stitch to secure the loop in place. Work as frequently as directed in the pattern.

Stuffing and sewing

All the flowers are made using the same basic structure. You will have a body and head piece, then two ARMS and two LEGS. The head of each flower then becomes distinctive with the petals that complete them. Each flower requires various techniques; some are worked directly onto the head and others are made separately and then sewn on, so follow the specifics within the pattern. If you use a centraliser stitch marker as you make your BODY/HEAD piece, then you will find it easy to mark the centre of your head to begin to position your petals.

ORDER OF SEWING

1. Stuff the BODY/HEAD and gather the stitches on the bottom of the body to close.
2. Gather and secure the tip of the ARMS, add a pinch of stuffing to them and sew across the top to close.
3. Repeat for the LEGS, adding a little more stuffing.
4. Using your centraliser marker on the body, lie your BODY/HEAD flat on its back and position the ARMS either side into the neckline. I recommend sewing down one side and then the other so that they are very securely attached.
5. Position the LEGS on the circle of the bottom at the angle shown in the photo opposite and oversew into position in the same way as the ARMS.
6. Use the techniques in the next few pages to assemble or add the petals to this basic shape.

GATHERING STITCHES

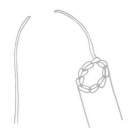

1   Fasten off the last stitch of the round by cutting the yarn and pulling the tail through the remaining loop.

2   Thread the end of the yarn onto a sewing needle and sew a running stitch through all the remaining stitches of the round.

3   Pull tightly to gather and close the stitches, then fasten off into the fabric around a stitch.

Assembling petals

After your BODY/HEAD and limbs are stuffed and assembled, complete the flowers with all the other details. It can be difficult to sew dozens of small pieces such as flowers or petals into position, so I have used a few different techniques to avoid this whenever possible. All flowers fall into the following technique categories:

HOODS AND COLLARS
(see photo page 155)

For flowers with collars or hoods it is essential to place the head through the opening at the neck before stuffing the body and head piece. You can then proceed as normal with the order of sewing.

Bluebell
Carnation
Crocus
Petunia
Winter Aconite

CHAIN LINES
(see illustration page 53)

The Foxglove and Heather have lots of smaller flowers that are attached to the head using a chain stitch to minimise the sewing up required and guarantee straighter lines of blooms. Sew all the ends into the individual pieces first, then using the colour used to make the head, slip stitch into the back of each piece and the head with chains in between, as detailed in the pattern.

Foxglove
Heather

RING OF PETALS ①

The petals are crocheted together into a ring, which is then placed onto the head. The specifics are detailed in each pattern, as they vary according to the size and shape of the petals. Some flowers also have chain stitches between the petals to space them correctly, and some two rings. Once you have created the ring, place it around the head from the front and then secure it by sewing around the edge through the adjoining crochet stitches or chain.

Alstroemeria
Clematis
Daffodil
Dahlia
Echinacea
Fuchsia
Gerbera
Iris
Lily
Poppy
Primrose
Snowdrop
Sunflower

SEWN FLOWERS ②

These flowers have a flower head made up of lots of individual smaller flowers. It is simpler to use the yarn ends from making them to sew them directly onto the head.

Allium
Hyacinth
Hydrangea

UPRIGHT PETALS ③

Flowers with upright heads have petals that you sew into place across the 'face' before sewing the eyes onto the front-facing petal rather than the head. For best results, position and sew this front petal on first before overlapping the others around the other sides.

Peony
Rose
Tulip

WORKED INTO HEAD ④

This group requires you to stuff and sew up before crocheting the petals directly onto the head, working your hook through the fabric.

Chrysanthemum
French Lavender
Marigold
Ranunculus

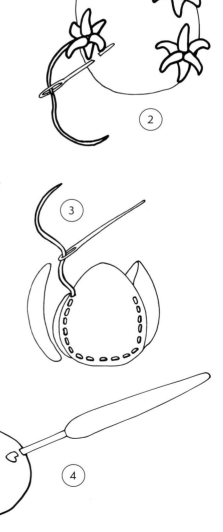

Adding slip stitch detail

SLIP STITCH CHAINS

 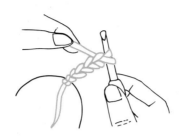 

1   Insert the hook through the fabric at the desired position, yarn over and pull through the fabric.

2   Chain the number of stitches stated in the pattern.

3   Working back down the chain, insert the hook into the next stitch, yarn over and pull through the stitch and the loop on the hook (one slip stitch made). Continue slip stitching down the chain, ending with just one loop on the hook.

SLIP STITCH TRAVERSE

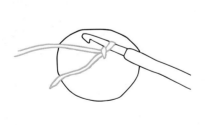 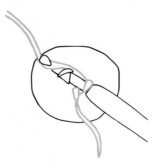 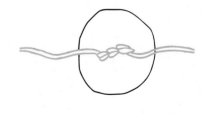

1   Insert the hook through the fabric at the desired position, yarn over and pull through the fabric.

2   Repeat step 1, moving across the surface of the fabric in the desired direction, being sure not to pull too tight to avoid puckering.

3   This can be used as a way of travelling across the fabric surface without having to break the yarn between slip stitch chains. These stitches may also be purely decorative.

Embroidering eyes and other details

I have embroidered eyes on to all the flowers using TOFT DK yarn in Cream and Black. Use your centraliser HEAD/BODY marker as a guide to find the centre of the head if you choose to add them before the petals, or on a flower such as the Rose, where you are adding them on top of the flower rather than into the centre.

1. Secure Cream yarn at the top of the desired eye position.
2. Sew into the fabric two rounds down, one stitch across and back down into the original hole.
3. Complete the triangle shape in Cream and fasten off.
4. Using Black, sew two wraps in the centre of the triangle.

If wishing to use safety eyes, don't forget to add them before gathering your stitches on the bottom of the body but after stuffing the head. This can be a little fiddly as you will need to push them through the head fabric and then reach up through the body to secure the backs before stuffing and closing the whole part. Remember that you do not need to add eyes to your flower, but equally you might want to consider adding further characterisation, such as a small mouth. This can be done easily with just a few embroidered stitches in Black.

FURTHER EMBROIDERY

As on the Alstroemeria, it is possible to add further pattern and detail to your flowers by embroidering simple lines onto the petals or foliage. Use contrasting colours for bold markings, or use the same colour to create more texture on the ARMS.

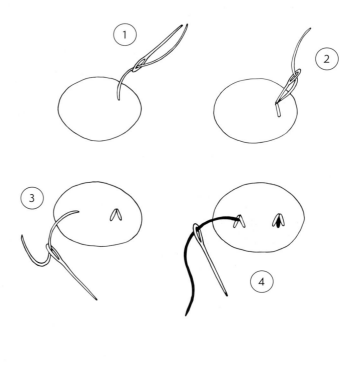

Displaying and gifting your flowers

DISPLAYING YOUR FLOWERS

Alexandra's Garden is always in season, and these flowers will brighten up your kitchen, lounge and every windowsill in your house all year long. Whether you are naturally green fingered or not, you can enjoy learning more about these flowers as you crochet them and display them in pride of place in your home in lieu of cut flowers that quickly fade.

In this book I have used various vases, jugs and pots to stand the flowers in. Those measuring 25cm high are ideal for displaying single flowers, especially on sideboards and shelves.

SYMBOLIC GIFTING

Flower symbolism became very significant during the Victorian era, when the declaration of emotions often had to go unsaid. It became a belief that flowers could embody and represent deep emotions, thoughts and feelings, and so gifting flowers to others to express yourself became very popular. Although today the significance of many of these flowers may no longer be so well known, the messages you can convey to the recipient of your crocheted flowers can go far beyond red roses of love.

JOIN THE COMMUNITY

Share your flower pictures with the TOFT community using #alexsgarden and #croyourown. If you need any help with the techniques in this book, get in touch @toft_uk and we will point you to a video to ensure you can get your flower to bloom as boldly as the ones on these pages.

TOFT's crochet range extends well beyond the fence at the bottom of the garden, and you can find more plant kits, subscriptions and information about events on our social media pages.

For all materials, tools and to see our worldwide yarn stockists, visit www.toftuk.com.

Thanks

My thanks begin this time with Edward and Alex. Ever since the day I let others know I was pregnant, I have been asked, 'What will you make for Alex?', and I really didn't know the answer until the first UK COVID-19 lockdown of 2020. Without their strength and continuous giggling, despite the uncertainty and challenges around them, this book would never have been made and I would never have found the love of another hobby. Over the last few years we have made some brilliant memories in our garden and I know that mud, manure and mulching are now part of our lives forever. With further thanks to Farah for taking it to the next level, with her expertise on perfect edges, rye grass and rear-rollers, and the shared pursuit of the perfect English country garden.

Of course, as this project developed over a long stretch of time, many hooks were involved, reworking the flowers in as many colours as we could imagine.

Special thanks to:

Rachel Critchley, for her expertise and attention to detail in checking all the technical details of what is my most diverse collection of patterns to date. And for her tireless quest (with the help of Jess Leese) for the best vintage pastels, and for making sure the TOFT warehouse is full to the brim with Green forever more.

Evie Birch, for a week making the first few petals, for her step-by-step illustrations of all the techniques we used to make them, and then for a whole year of getting excited to pack thousands of flower kits during the pandemic.

Further thanks to the whole TOFT team past and present, without whom none of this would be possible, but specifically:

Beth Plumbley, for being there the first time we turned my kitchen into a florist, and for the stamina involved in making the photos in this book so beautiful.

Natasha Jackson, for never tiring of the request for 'just eight more like that', and for bringing a smile to every challenge.

A big thanks to the extra speedy hooks of Rosie Collins, Jess Leese, Liz Kidner, Yantra Taneva, Emma Chamberlain and Annabel Cox.

Photography was by Yantra Taneva, Denitsa Raykova, Rosie Collins and Nathasja Vermaning (who always had a sunflower in her suitcase). A special thanks to Yantra, for making the photographs capture TOFT yarn perfectly, and Rosie, for having the patience to create the perfect charts and graphics for each petal.